HISTORIAN AND SCIENTIST

HISTORIAN AND SCIENTIST
AN ESSAY ON THE NATURE OF HISTORY
AND THE SOCIAL SCIENCES

BY

GAETANO SALVEMINI

Essay Index Reprint Series

BOOKS FOR LIBRARIES PRESS
FREEPORT, NEW YORK

STANDARD BOOK NUMBER:

8369-1049-4

LIBRARY OF CONGRESS CATALOG CARD NUMBER:

75-80396

PRINTED IN THE UNITED STATES OF AMERICA

TO THE MEMORY OF
LAURO DE BOSIS

PREFACE

THE reader will find in the pages that follow the text of four lectures delivered in December 1938 at the University of Chicago. The printed form preserves the informal and colloquial style in which the lectures were given. The only changes are the insertion of a few examples here and there and the addition of a section on the sources of historical knowledge.

The author wishes to thank President Hutchins of the University of Chicago and Dean Redfield of the Division of Social Sciences for giving him the privilege of addressing an intelligent and responsive audience.

While the lectures delivered at the University of Chicago sum up an experience in historical research going back, alas, almost half a century, the lecture "What is Culture?" which has been added as an appendix gives the gist of what the author has learned in his practical career as a teacher. He hopes that in publishing his reflections on this subject he will help some young teacher to free himself from the prejudice of the necessity for encylopedic knowledge

—a mortal disease which in present-day schools and colleges is undermining the intellectual health of both teachers and pupils.

GAETANO SALVEMINI

Cambridge, Massachusetts
May, 1939

CONTENTS

I
A DEFINITION OF TERMS

I

A DEFINITION OF TERMS

LET us take as the starting point of our discussion of history and the social sciences the Aristotelian doctrine according to which intellectual activity is either scientific — if it aims at the ascertainment of truth; or aesthetic — if it has as its goal poetical creation; or practical — if it is directed toward action.

Leonardo da Vinci was an artist when he painted the "Last Supper" and a scientist when he drew the anatomy of the human body. A politician who addresses the electorate, recounting his own achievements, is a man of action who aims at the solution of a practical problem, namely, that of getting votes. He therefore falls under Aristotle's third heading, though he may, at times, display the most amazing gifts of poetical imagination and although even the most supercilious scientist is bound to admit that, at times, his statements are quite true.

Thus I shall term "science" all endeavor to ascertain facts and their interrelations.

Coming now to the definition of history, I shall term "history" all endeavor to reconstruct past events with the help of their remnants or of the traces which they have left in human memory.

In common parlance many investigations which aim at the reconstruction of the past do not fall under the heading of history. The astronomer who collects from all periods and all countries data on which to tabulate heavenly phenomena; the geologist who, basing his research on the distribution and stratification of minerals in the earth's crust, tries to deduct therefrom the phases through which the earth has passed before assuming its present aspect; the paleontologist who, with the help of fossil remains, re-creates flora and fauna which became extinct thousands of years ago; the naturalist who investigates the origin of species — all these are called scientists, while the name "historian" is applied only to those scholars who devote themselves to reconstructing the past of the human race. As a matter of fact, there is no essential difference between the problems which confront the scientist in reconstructing the astronomic, geological, or biological past and the problems which confront the historian in reconstructing the human past. In both cases the expert reconstructs the past with the help of the evidence which the past has left behind it. The technique used by the various investigators may differ, inasmuch as they have to devise different expedients to fit the different sources of information at their disposal, but the method of extracting information from sources remains the same, because the human mind in all circumstances works in accordance with the same laws of thought.

In reconstructing the past we can set before ourselves two different aims: we can limit ourselves to ascertaining the facts one by one; or we can ask ourselves whether there exists a connection of cause and effect between preceding and subsequent facts. Disconnected facts have no interest in themselves. They were all born free and equal. Facts begin to acquire significance only when they are grouped in a system of cause and effect. Only then does knowledge contribute to wisdom.

The work which stops short at the ascertainment of isolated facts about the past we call erudition, and we designate as historians those scholars who seek to organize these facts according to the principle of causality. The work of Le Nain de Tillemont, who in the seventeenth century industriously collected all the sources of information then available on the Roman emperors, selected from them the most reliable data, with all the necessary critical precautions, and then compiled the annals of the Roman Empire, is a work of erudition. Gibbon, who, utilizing the erudition of Le Nain de Tillemont, described the causes and the phases of the decline of the Roman Empire, was an historian. Erudition prepares bricks for the historian. The historian is the architect.

From erudition and from history so defined let us now pass to the definition of the social sciences. I say "social sciences" because this is the term adopted by the social scientists themselves to designate their studies. But the subject of the present discussion is precisely whether or not the social sciences are really sciences. For the time being, I shall make use of the terms "social sciences" and "social scientists" in a provisional way. Pending the results of our discussion, I beg the reader to place in imagination a question mark between brackets after these formulas each time I use them.

The division between history and the social sciences is generally regarded as a pure matter of dates. The historian is one who deals with the study of events of which there are no longer living witnesses, whereas the social scientist deals with contemporary events, about which he can make direct personal observation. A book on the French Revolution is classed as history, while one on the Russian Revolution of 1917 is generally regarded as a contribution to the social sciences. One who studies the organization of the family in ancient Rome is an historian; one who studies the organization of the family in a negro tribe of the present day is regarded as a social scientist.

On closer scrutiny, however, this conception proves not to fit the facts. One who studies contemporary events derives only an infinitesimal part of his information from immediate personal knowledge. The greater part of his material comes to him from the testimony of others. Every witness, whether dead or living, may have made mistakes or may have had the intention of misleading. All testimony must therefore be subjected to a scrutiny both of its accuracy and of its sincerity. This is equally indispensable whether we use the history of Herodotus to reconstruct the Persian Wars, or the memoirs of Trotsky to study events in

Russia in 1917. Abundant official statistics are published today, and statistics belong to the realm of the social sciences. But many of these statistics, when subjected to the methods of historical criticism, are useful only as a proof that in our century the sources of poetical imagination have not dried up.

If history is the reconstruction of the past, even events contemporary to ourselves belong to the past. The speech made in Congress yesterday belongs to the past. The notes taken by a journalist during the speech are records of this past. One who uses these notes, be he historian or social scientist, must make sure whether or not the journalist gave a faithful reproduction of the speech, *i.e.*, whether, at the moment of taking down his notes and editing them for the press, he misunderstood or even intentionally misreported the speaker's address by ascribing to him statements he never made. This critical inquiry is indispensable whether we are dealing with a speech made yesterday at Washington and published today in a daily newspaper, or whether we are studying the Philippics of Demosthenes.

The line of division between history and the social sciences is not one of chronology. It results from the different aims pursued by the historian and the social scientist.

When one investigates family organization in a given country, at a given time, what factors determined that organization and what fresh circumstances transformed it, one is doing a piece of historical research, no matter whether the type of family belongs to the past or to the present. If one uses all the historical information available about different types of family organization in the greatest possible number of countries and periods, in order to determine whether or not there are constant features which may be formulated into laws, then one is working on a problem of social science.

The astronomer, in so far as he collects evidence about heavenly phenomena observed in the past, is doing the work of an historian, but in so far as he determines periodicity, *i.e.*, the laws obtaining among these phenomena, he is doing work analogous to that of the social scientist in the domain of human relations. The study of historical data and the working out of laws are intermingled in astronomy. In the study of human relations there is a division of labor between history, which reconstructs the facts, and the social sciences, which devote themselves to detecting uniformities and deducting laws therefrom.

The historian often jumps to the formulation of laws on the basis of facts ascertained by history; on the other hand, the social scientist is or should feel obliged personally to test facts before formulating laws. But for the sake of our discussion I shall keep the work of the historian distinct from that of the social scientist, though they often overlap, and I shall include under the heading of "history" all investigations aiming at re-creating the past without pretense at determining laws, and under the heading of "social sciences" all attempts to determine the laws of human behavior.

II
INTELLECTUAL HYBRIDS

II

INTELLECTUAL HYBRIDS

WHILE definitions and classifications are
indispensable, they are also dangerous.
They are indispensable if the mind is not to
lose itself in a chaos of disconnected snapshots
and if our discussions are not to be bogged in a
mire of mischievous misunderstandings, fruitless wranglings, and equivocal conclusions.
The mind has to find its bearings in the maze
of objects. Without definitions and classifications, facts would form an inextricable jumble.
On the other hand, definitions and classifications are dangerous because they are but abstract patterns created by the mind for its
practical needs. They select from among the
connotations of objects which we wish to distinguish from one other only those connotations
which best suit our practical needs. They are
the results of a process of abstraction. After having worked out our abstract patterns we find
that each fact is like a solid with many facets
and that in defining it and classifying it with
other facts we have taken into account only a

few of its facets — often not more than one. Moreover, there exist crossbreeds in which the connotations of different abstract patterns are intermingled. These hybrids would strictly require new definitions. But in practice we classify each of them under the general type with which it has the greatest number of features in common. Thus confusions or doubts may arise, as in the case of the baby who calls a horse with the word used to designate a dog because both horse and dog are quadrupeds, or as in the case of the lady librarian who was puzzled whether to catalogue a book on the Immaculate Conception under theology or embryology.

There are crossbreeds between historical activities and practical ones. The Philippics of Demosthenes overflow with information precious to historians. But Demosthenes did not aim at historical writing. He was a crusader who made use of historical material and of his gifts as an orator to induce the Athenians to assume an attitude of uncompromising resistance to Philip of Macedon. His orations fall under the heading of practical activities. The man of action may utilize material collected by the historian or social scientist for his practical purposes. But he is neither an historian nor a social scientist.

Another species of hybrid arises when the historian or the social scientist does not resist the temptation to couple his own moral judgment with the description of events or the formulation of laws. This was once considered to be one of the professional duties of the historian. "History," said Cicero, "is not only *lumen veritatis,* the light of truth, but also *magistra vitae,* the teacher of life." Today we believe that the historian, and with him the social scientist, must solve problems of facts and laws, and not of values.

What causes produced a given event? What results followed it? These are quantitative problems. Is a given action to be praised or censured? This is a qualitative problem. It belongs to the domain of the moralist and not of the historian or the social scientist. When they encroach upon the task of the moralist, the activities of the historian or social scientist fall under Aristotle's definition of practical activities. What is imperative is that the historian or social scientist should draw a line between the moments in which he is writing as a moralist and the moments in which his purpose is to impart information concerning the way things did and do happen.

Propaganda agents always introduce themselves as open-minded and impartial historians or social scientists; they are wolves in sheep's clothing. Nowadays the public finds it more and more difficult to distinguish propaganda from honest information. One almost asks oneself whether most books of history or social science are not sheer propaganda adorned with footnotes. But I can name at least four Americans, no longer living, who are worthy to be called historians: Henry Charles Lea, author of *The History of the Inquisition in the Middle Ages;* Frederick Jackson Turner, author of *The Frontier in American History;* Edward Raymond Turner, author of *The Privy Council in England in the Seventeenth and Eighteenth Centuries;* and Charles Homer Haskins, author of *The Normans in European History.* These were true historians whom no one would dare term propaganda agents. Adam Smith was not a propaganda agent but an honest social scientist when he wrote *The Wealth of Nations,* since he gave what he honestly thought to be the truth, even though he may have been misled. When I discuss whether history and the social sciences are sciences I ask the reader to think of seekers for truth and not of propaganda agents.

There are also crossbreeds between historical works and works of art. In an historical novel like *The Three Musketeers* by Alexandre Dumas, *père,* a few facts drawn from historical sources are mingled with a great number of imaginative events and form a work of art. No one would quarrel with Dumas even if the three musketeers had never existed in real life. Just as there are historical novels, there are also scientific novels, such as those of Jules Verne and H. G. Wells; and, just as science does not become art simply because there are artists who use scientific knowledge as material for the constructions of their imagination, so history does not become art just because there are novelists who take the same liberties with the past as other artists do with the data of immediate experience.

Literary biographies such as the *Queen Victoria* of Lytton Strachey differ from the historical novel in that they are based on a closer adherence to historical sources. The characters and the situations are never imaginary; the starting point of the imagination is always a fact drawn from some historical document. However, the imagination works with a freedom to which the historian is not entitled. The historian must confine himself to constructing only those hypotheses which are made necessary by the incompleteness of the material, whereas the literary biographer adds hypotheses of the second and third degree which are not in themselves improbable but are unsupported by documentary proof. Literary biographies are undoubtedly more thrilling and fascinating than any work of history, and more effective in diffusing historical knowledge among the public at large. But all the same they are not historical works. They are more or less successful crossbreeds between history and art.

There exist works of history which are also works of art. But these are not hybrids, nor should they be classified under the category of artistic activities. Lucidity, color, vivacity, a form closely molded to the contour of the facts, these gifts are highly desirable in all products of intellectual activity. Tyndall's book on glaciers and those of Fabre on the lives of insects are first-rate works of science and at the same time fine works of art. Tyndall and Fabre are scientists; they aimed at scientific description and not at artistic creation.

The photographer who takes the picture of a person performs the work of an historian. This is also true of the artist who paints a portrait of the same person. The artist, however, does not limit himself to the mechanical reproduction of the physical features of the person but seeks rather to reveal his character by omitting irrelevant details and concentrating on essential features. By selection, he produces an historical work of higher caliber than that of the photographer. But his work when portraying a real person is not in the same category with the work he produces when painting an imaginary subject. Raphael, in painting the portrait of Pope Julius II, did the work of an historian even if it was at the same time a great work of art; on the other hand, in painting his Madonnas he produced works of art but not historical works. Nobody asks whether his Madonna resembles the historical mother of Christ and wife of Joseph. But we all want to be certain that Raphael really gave us the Julius II of fact. Without this certitude the thoughts associated with the portrait of Julius II would be inhibited by doubts. From the historical standpoint we should prefer to an inaccurate portrait painted by the great artist some other portrait painted by a mediocre artist, provided we were certain he had done his best to give us at least the physical features of the original.

Hence we may repeat with Shelley that "every good historian is a poet," on condition that we interpret these words not in the sense that every good historian is nothing *but* a poet, but in the sense that every good historian is not only an historian but *also* a poet.

However, the essential element of history is the ascertaining of facts. If the historian happens to be an artist in addition, all the better. His public, while not rejecting aesthetic emotions, demands from him, above all else, correct information, and to the fascinating novels of Walter Scott they prefer the unadorned but critically sound writings of Mr. Coulton on medieval England. This is why, when reading Strachey's books, we are continually uneasy — we never feel certain whether his statements are the duly extracted gist of historical sources or the purposely created figments of his imagination. Rather than swallow such a crossbreed of history and romance, I prefer to enjoy *The Three Musketeers* of Alexandre Dumas. This work never aspires to being taken as an historical work, and wishes only to amuse; it succeeds admirably in its purpose because the reader can surrender to the magic of the author's imagination without being disturbed by doubts concerning the truth of what he reads.

Then are history and the social sciences — so defined and distinguished from hybrids — really sciences?

III

AN ISSUE WHICH CANNOT BE EVADED

III

AN ISSUE WHICH CANNOT BE EVADED

THIS discussion is not prompted merely by a desire for hairsplitting. Underlying it is the question whether the work of the historian and social scientist can open up to the community fresh opportunities for furthering justice, well-being, and happiness.

Many historians and social scientists, engrossed in their specialized fields, have no ears for the discussions going on outside their classrooms about the practical usefulness of their specialties. Others unhesitatingly settle the question to suit themselves and go their way unperturbed, in the conviction that any discussion of the scientific character of their activity is superfluous since its scientific character cannot be questioned. Others take up an attitude of hurt dignity and declare that they cannot be expected to concern themselves with vulgar matters of practical utility. They pursue their labors for the same reasons that a poet writes his poems, or non-professional sportsmen play football, *i.e.,* for the joy of intellectual adventure and of asserting their own personalities. "I write for my own pleasure," they repeat with Flaubert. Their disinterested activities may contribute to the well-being, happiness, and freedom from boredom of others. But such practical results are a matter of indifference to the man who dwells on the lofty summits of the intellect. The eagle does not pay heed to sparrows. A scholar is not a Philistine.

I am far from denying that the pleasure of disinterested intellectual work is the finest privilege granted to the scholar. Were I to be reborn, I should ask to be again endowed with this privilege, even though I should once more spend my life in that economic category which statisticians define as the "recipients of low incomes." However, it is one thing to say that the scholar must be left free in his work without being obliged to transmute its results into dollars and cents; it is quite another matter to pronounce that the community has no right to expect practical utility from the work of scholars.

The munificent donor or the statesman who founds a university or library knowing that a certain number of persons in it will dedicate their lives to historical studies and the social sciences does not take this step for the simple pleasure of providing those persons with the joy of disinterested intellectual adventure. Were history and the social sciences dependent on nothing more than a philanthropic impulse of that nature, I fear that the departments of history and political science in our universities would be no more numerous than those departments where poets might be taught how to pen verses, with the result that historians and social scientists would have to live on an even narrower margin than poets.

A university lacking in departments of history and social science would be like a body stripped of some vital organ. Why is this so? The reasons are two in number.

The first reason operates to the advantage of historical studies. Through the medium of historical studies we seek to learn about our social, moral, and intellectual origins, just as by means of the physical sciences we learn the conditions of our organic life. Directly or indirectly, all historical research aims at solving the basic problem of knowing how some present situation has come to be as it is. From the thinkers of the nineteenth century we have inherited the conviction that the tissue of ideas, words, institutions, religious rites, customs, arts, sciences, which enveloped us at birth and with which we live surrounded, was woven by our ancestors through the effort of centuries. Our present day is not for us a system of forces improvised out of the void the day before yesterday and destined to melt away under the influence of other forces which will unexpectedly crop up the day after tomorrow. Our present day is the product of a social, moral, and intellectual evolution whose origins are lost in the mists of time, and will in its turn be the necessary condition of future developments. From this conviction arises the fact that knowledge of the present dissociated from knowledge of the past could never satisfy our curiosity. History has become a primary category of our thought, an *a priori* according to which our experience groups itself. The historical sense is a kind of sixth sense which we cannot fail to acquire as we breathe the intellectual atmosphere of our times. To a large extent "Know thyself" means today "Seek the origins of thyself in the past."

The second reason explains the interest evinced by the community in the development

of the social sciences. It is based on the hope
that sooner or later the laws — if such exist —
to which social phenomena conform will be
discovered, and that knowledge of those laws
will help us to regulate our conduct more in-
telligently. Only if we succeed in discovering
the laws of social life — assuming them to exist — can we save ourselves fruitless efforts and
disastrous mistakes. These laws — always assuming they exist — cannot be revealed to us
either by transcendental authority or by any
metaphysics, whether ancient or modern,
claiming to deduce the solution of all problems from magic formulas expressing the so-
called "nature of things." The laws of social
life cannot be determined except by the method
followed during the past three centuries by the
sciences of the physical world — that is, by examining the greatest possible number of facts;
coördinating them in accordance with their
coexistence in space, their succession in time,
and the principle of causality; classifying the
various groups of facts according to constant
similarities and dissimilarities; and expressing
these constant similarities and dissimilarities in
synthetic formulas, *i.e.*, laws which enable us
to predict that the appearance of a given phe-

nomenon will be the signal for the appearance of other phenomena indissolubly connected with the first.

Practical interests are not to be looked upon by the scholar with contempt. Geometry arose from the need of measuring agricultural land. Scientific astronomy was primarily developed from the practical need of adjusting the calendar. The development of geography was bound up with commercial interests. The invention of firearms gave rise to the study of the laws of motion: the wars and sieges of the sixteenth century acted as laboratories of experimental mechanics and paved the way for the discoveries of Galileo, Huygens, and Newton. Hydrostatics was suggested to Italian engineers of the sixteenth and seventeenth centuries by the need of controlling the rivers of northern Italy. Pasteur's investigations in biology were undertaken to meet the interests of silkworm cultivators and wine dealers.

Of this twofold hope of a practical nature — that is to say, the hope that history may reveal to us our origins, and the hope that the social sciences may reveal to us the laws of social life — is born the almost religious zeal for historical and social studies which characterizes our age. This same hope explains why we feel the need of discussing our methods of research, the soundness of the materials on which we work, and the reliability of our conclusions. This explains why many historians and social scientists ask themselves: "Are history and the social sciences really sciences?" Can the community expect from our labor a sure knowledge of its own past and hence of itself, the discovery of laws to which human activities must conform, and the formulation of practical rules which are not merely empirical? Or is there no hope that our efforts will some day succeed in seizing upon objective reality, and must history and the social sciences be forever condemned to producing either figments of the imagination, pleasant or otherwise, or else dishonest propaganda?

A well-known story is that of the English historian of the eighteenth century who while in prison for debt heard the sound of wrangling in the next corridor and tried to find out what had actually happened. The conflicting nature of the reports made it impossible for him to elicit the truth of the matter. He concluded that, since he was unable to ascertain what had happened a little while before at the very threshold of his own room, he could never learn what had happened in distant times and places. He therefore gave up writing history. Is the skepticism of that Britisher of tender conscience justified?

In this discussion history and the social sciences sink or swim together. The effort to ascertain constant similarities or dissimilarities between the facts or groups of facts furnished to the social sciences by historical research would be vain if the facts themselves offered no guarantee of their certainty. No solid building can be constructed with materials lacking the requisite consistence.

To determine whether revolutions are governed by constant laws, there is only one method: we must compare one with the other the greatest possible number of revolutions — let us say the religious revolution of the eleventh century, the revolutions of the Italian cities and of the cities of the Low Countries between the eleventh and the fifteenth century, the Protestant Revolution, the English Revolution of the seventeenth century, the American Revolution of the eighteenth century, the French Revolution, the Russian Revolution — and we must see whether between these phenomena so far apart in time and space there can be discovered similarities or dissimilarities which are constant. These labors will be successful only in so far as the specialized historical works we use can be relied upon. If the facts or groups of facts to be correlated have been arbitrarily described and grouped by the historian, the labors of the social scientist are likewise doomed to failure. A law — that is to say, a formula describing the constant behavior of a group of phenomena — is valid only in so far as the phenomena on which it is based have been correctly ascertained.

In discussing the problem of whether history and the social sciences are sciences, I renounce all pretensions to elevating myself above the humble ground of common sense to the lofty spheres of philosophy. Not that the desire to rise to such levels is lacking in me; I have simply not the capacity. At those altitudes the atmosphere is too rarified for my lungs and heart. In the writings of many philosophers of our day in spite of every effort I understand not one single thing. Their works seem to me to be fog factories. They produce on my mind the effect of inverted filters: when I begin reading, my ideas are clear; but when I have finished they have become so turbid that, if I ask these philosophers a question and they kindly condescend to answer, the immediate result of their answer is that I no longer understand even my own question. In their profound thoughts I am unable to spot where they are right and where they are wrong. The fault lies, no doubt, with my weak intelligence; but I cannot help it.

So no revelation of epoch-making but obscure doctrines is to be expected from me. I shall expound my way of thinking as clearly as lies in my power. Clarity is the moral integrity of the mind. In my statements the reader will be able, I hope, instantly to detect where my reasoning goes wrong.

IV

THE SOURCES OF HISTORICAL KNOWLEDGE

THE SOURCES OF HISTORICAL KNOWLEDGE

THE evidence which the past has left behind it, and through which the historian reconstructs it, falls into two categories: *remains* and *records*.

Remains are fragments of the past which chance has preserved down to the present: minerals, fossils, rudimentary or atrophied survivals of once active and vital organs in creatures living today, bones of men and animals, weapons, utensils, old buildings, graves, paintings, sculpture, religious rites, addresses, controversies, letters, philosophical treatises, etc.

Records are those works of the human intelligence which have been created with the deliberate purpose of preserving the memory of events: monuments, inscriptions, portraits, documents, historical sources in the narrower sense of the term.

Records again fall into two categories: *documents* and *reports*.

A *document* is a record whose exactitude is

guaranteed by special formalities: the intervention of public officials, the presence of witnesses, the signatures of the interested parties, initial and final formulas, the appending of seals. Under this heading fall international treaties, deeds of sale and purchase, wills, official records of trials, inquests, parliamentary debates, and so forth.

Reports are narratives, made either by eyewitnesses or by people who obtained their information from eyewitnesses, dating from times more or less distant from the events. They include autobiographies, biographies, chronicles, inscriptions on tombstones or other objects, commemorative monuments, portraits, sculptured or painted, etc.

The paintings, sculpture, buildings, poetry, and letters of Michelangelo are *remains*. They give us his activities exactly as they left his mind in the first half of the sixteenth century. The historian of art may err more or less in utilizing these remains for his purposes. But the works of Michelangelo still continue to exist, and anyone can resort to them to check the scholar's statements. The ruins of Pompeii are a fragment of a Roman city as it existed in the year 79 A.D. There is no barrier in this instance between the scholar of today and the objects of his study. In examining them, the historian finds himself in direct contact with the past. He works in the same way as the physiologist studying an organ, as the chemist analyzing a substance, as the astronomer observing a star.

It is true that remains of the past have very rarely come down to us in a perfect state of preservation. They have suffered nearly always from the ravages of the elements or of men. They have often been tampered with or even fabricated by forgers. To the historian falls the task of restoring the remains in their original form and of detecting forgeries. Mistakes have often been made and will always be made. But modern technique can be justly proud of its achievements in this field.

When the historian has to reconstitute the past with the aid of documents, he is in a less favorable position. A document claims to be an exact picture of a past event. Nay, more, it is itself an essential part of that event. Until the document is complete with all necessary legal formalities, the transaction, whether it be a sale, a will, a contract, a sentence, an international treaty, remains null and void. Nevertheless, between the historian and the event recorded by the document there intervenes the activity of those whose intention it was to transmit the memory of the event by means of the document. And wherever the human will consciously transmits the record of a fact there is a possibility of error or of intentional deception. There are forged documents like the famous Donation of Constantine, which according to the most accredited hypothesis was concocted in the Papal Court during the eighth century. An international treaty published in the press may be accompanied by secret clauses, the knowledge of which would practically reverse the apparent meaning of the treaty. The collections of diplomatic documents which Foreign Offices from time to time issue to justify their activities are as a rule more or less skillful forgeries. Documents of different dates are merged into one single document; a document of a day or an hour is attributed to another day or another hour; essential documents are mutilated and others altogether suppressed so that those which are published acquire a false significance. The "yellow book" which in the Summer of 1914 the French Foreign Office published on the events leading to the outbreak of the World War is a classical example of this kind of mystification. Again, a document may be authentic and yet not truthful. The parties who go before a notary to draw up a deed of sale with all due formalities may have agreed to the insertion of a price which does not correspond to the sum actually paid, or may have even connived in a bogus rate. In June 1902 the Italian Foreign Minister pledged his Government not to participate in a war of aggression against France, and left the Paris Cabinet a free hand in Morocco. In return the French Government left the Italians a free hand in Libya. The notes embodying those agreements were given a false date, November 2, of that year, and under this false date they were published in 1919. In other words, when the historian is working with remains he only needs to make sure that they are authentic. Once this work has been accomplished, he has come into direct contact with a fragment of the past. But when he is dealing with a document it is not enough to ascertain its authenticity. There is the further task of detecting whether the document contains false statements due to error or to deliberate bad faith on the part of those who drew it up. As a general rule, however, an authentic document may be taken as an accurate and truthful record of the event of which it transmits the memory, unless definite grounds for suspicion appear. When one works with documents, one is working on a basis which is slightly less firm than that of remains.

The situation changes for the worse when the historian has to deal with reports. In this case the guarantees of accuracy possessed by documents are lacking. If the report is the work of an eyewitness, the reliability of the description depends entirely on the trustworthiness of the witness. We possess on the Bolshevik Revolution, of which Russia was the scene in 1917, and on the conditions in Russia from 1917 onwards a large library of reports of all kinds; but the historical value of this material is slight; the greater part of it is tainted with party spirit, personal passions, bad faith, more or less fanatical propaganda for or against Bolshevism.

Still worse is our position in regard to reports which come to us not from eyewitnesses but from intermediaries between us and the primary sources which no longer exist. Each one of these intermediaries was subject to error of interpretation or may have intentionally distorted his source's statements. Had the Moses of Michelangelo been lost and had nothing remained but a copy on a small scale made by a mediocre artist, this document would give us a very imperfect idea of the original. But we should be still worse off if all we had was a description of the original made by a man of letters. The longer the chain of intermediaries intervening between the event and ourselves, the greater the probability of error or of misrepresentation.

Reports which have enjoyed centuries of undisputed authority have been revealed as of very slight value. All serious historians are convinced today that the account which Livy gives of the origins of Rome is in a large measure legendary, and that many assertions of Tacitus concerning the first period of the Roman Empire must be taken with a grain of salt.

The fewer the reports on which the historian can base his investigations, the less and less favorable the position. What, for instance, is the historical value of the commentaries on the Gallic Wars left us by Julius Caesar? It is hardly probable that they have greater value than the memoirs of the army chiefs responsible for the battle of the Marne in 1914. But we can check the memoirs of the French army chiefs with those of the English and German chiefs. This is not possible with respect to Caesar's memoirs. The conquest of Gaul by Julius Caesar cannot be questioned, but we should do well not to swallow blindly all that Julius Caesar wrote.

There are vast periods of the past for which the historical sources are so fragmentary that little or nothing can be gleaned from them to dispel our ignorance. To cite an example, the size of the population is one of the basic factors to be taken into consideration in explaining social phenomenon. But as to the population of Greece and of the Near East before the Roman conquest, we know nothing. At most, we can advance plausible hypotheses on the population of a given city, like Athens, and of a given country, like Egypt, and this only for a few centuries. As to the population of the Roman Empire, given the scarcity of the sources, it is not possible to arrive at a safe conclusion; we can only hold that in the first two centuries after Christ the population must have been larger than in the third century and the centuries immediately following it. Even in respect to the population of the city of Rome we can only build up hypotheses and make guesses. For the early Middle Ages we know nothing except that the population must have been much less numerous than that of more recent centuries. We have almost no sure data on the population of the most civilized countries of Europe before the fourteenth century. These examples of insurmountable ignorance might be multiplied.

For other periods of history we have more abundant information, in the form not only of reports but also of remains and documents; these remains and documents permit us to check the accuracy and truthfulness of the reports; and this enables us to reconstruct many of the events with certitude, not only in outline but in a considerable amount of detail. As we approach modern times the number of historical sources increases. But this very abundance becomes a fresh source of difficulty: anyone who tried to read at first hand all the sources for the history of the French Revolution would have time to live and die several times over before he succeeded in reconstructing those events.

V

HISTORICAL SKEPTICISM

HISTORICAL SKEPTICISM

ALL this is true. But it only means that the historian has not an easy task. When the difficulty arises from a superabundance of sources, as is the case for these last centuries, and still more so for events contemporaneous with ourselves, it is quite possible to select the essential sources and ignore the rest or keep them in reserve for the elucidation of special points. And when he cannot solve a given problem for lack of sources, the historian confesses his ignorance and stops there. All scientists do the same. When we say that the aim of history is to state "what has actually happened," we do not mean "*all* that has actually happened in all times and in all places"; we mean "what has actually happened in the field on which our attention is focused and for which we have a sufficient wealth of information."

Ignorance is no ground for skepticism. If it were so, no science would escape skepticism. As late as the first half of the nineteenth century the sources of the Nile were unknown. This did not mean that the sources of all rivers were unknown or that geographers were not scientists because they were as yet unable to trace the sources of the Nile. The origins of cancer still constitute a baffling mystery. This is not a reason for us to consider as unfounded the knowledge we now have of the origins and cure of diphtheria, meningitis, and malaria. The languages of ancient Crete and Etruria are still mysterious, but the deciphering of hieroglyphics and of cuneiform characters, the reconstruction of ancient life in the Near East through archaeological excavations, the creation *ex novo* of Egyptian economic history with the help of the papyri, and many other marvelous achievements of contemporary historical research, are as secure and well founded as the conquests which have been made by the more exact among the sciences.

Here I may be warned that the English historian of the eighteenth century who gave up writing historical works was concerned not with events of which he could not get any records but with events on which there were many conflicting records. His skepticism arose from the fact that he was unable to find out which was the correct one.

In discussing this point let us first of all draw a distinction between the difficulty which arises when facts have to be established and those disagreements which arise when a moral judgment is passed on those facts. In 1792 the monarchical form of government was abolished and a republic established in France. French monarchists are of the opinion that this was a crime and still weep on account of it. French Republicans are of the opinion that it was well done. This controversy will continue forever unabated. However, it has nothing to do with historical studies. It belongs to the field of practical activities. On the other hand, why and how was the monarchical form of government abolished in France at that time? And why at that particular time and not at some other time? And why in that way and not in some other way? And what were the immediate and the secondary consequences of that event? These are historical problems. On such problems historians often dispute. They are unable to agree on what actually happened.

If from history we shift to the social sciences doubtful theories are no less numerous. A typical example of a law which was accepted as dogma by almost all the intellectuals of the second half of the eighteenth century and of the entire nineteenth century, and which appears to us nowadays to be formulated on weak foundations, is that of indefinite progress. According to this law, mankind steadily advances from barbarism toward higher and higher states of civilization. To the question of what civilization is, no one has ever advanced a generally accepted answer; but, fundamentally, by civilization everyone means that condition of society which has now been attained by those countries of Europe and America which term themselves civilized, plus those improvements to which the most highly developed moral consciences in those countries aspire. As a matter of fact, there exists no people whose history can be described as a constant advance from a state of barbarism to that form of life which each one of us regards as "civilization." Many people have raised themselves to forms of life more or less approximating those which come up to our ideals, and then have ceased to advance, or have fallen back to those stages which had already been surpassed; some, after more or less long periods of lethargy and decadence, have experienced periods of revival and of advancement; others, once become decadent, have never risen again. The law of progress was constructed by the social scientists of the second half of the eighteenth century on a tenuous basis of facts, that is, on the experience only of the most civilized countries in Europe in the more recent centuries; it was almost universally accepted in the first half of the nineteenth century because it offered useful arguments to liberals in their struggle against despotic governments; and it still continues to be handed down simply by force of inertia. But every historian who tries to fit the history of a people or of all peoples into the framework of that supposed law realizes in the end that he has wasted his time in futile effort.

It is this category of doubtful issues or errors, and not disagreements on moral issues, that would justify skepticism in both history and the social sciences.

If, however, historical skepticism were right, every court of law would have to be closed. In a court of law, when his client is innocent, the counsel for the defense does the work of an historian. All he has to do is to lay the case before the jury as it really happened, with the relevant proofs. On the other hand, when the defendant is guilty, the aim of the defense counsel is to make him appear innocent, or at any rate as little guilty as possible. Instead of keeping to the true facts, the defense counsel builds up a case by ignoring or distorting such incriminating evidence as he can, and constructing specious theories to cover evidence that cannot be explained away. In this case the defense counsel is not an historian but a propaganda agent. The public prosecutor is paid by the community to ascertain the truth. His task should therefore be that of an historian. But this class of public officials is often afflicted by a sort of professional deterioration which makes them regard every defendant as guilty. Therefore there are jurymen whose task consists in weighing evidence and arguments and giving their verdict. Their task is that of the historian. They sometimes give a definite verdict of guilty or of not guilty, sometimes an open verdict; they may also err from time to time. But nobody in his right mind would maintain that law courts can never reach any verdict for lack of evidence or for an excessive amount of conflicting evidence.

The historian must assume, at one and the same time, the function of public prosecutor, counsel for the defense, and jury. He too may err. But this is no reason for asserting that all history departments should be closed down, while courts of law should remain open. This only means that historians and social scientists must be cautious if they want to avoid blundering. Are these not the danger and the duty of all scientists?

Pasteur traced all diseases to bacteria, whereas modern medicine traces many diseases to deficiencies in vitamins or derangement of organs. Was Pasteur not a scientist, and a great scientist at that, even if some of his theories are disputed, nay, more, have been proved incorrect?

Napoleon existed. Somebody has maintained that Napoleon is a solar myth, but no man of common sense ever took this doctrine seriously. Why? Because were we to deny the existence of Napoleon, we should no longer understand anything of all the documents from which we draw the history of the nineteenth century. If there is currency inflation, there will be a rise in prices. This, also, is an indisputable truth. Why? Because, were we to think differently, all we know about the results which currency inflation has always had in all times and in all countries, from the third century of the Roman Empire to our day, would suddenly be turned topsy-turvy.

VI

SELECTION AND IMAGINATION

VI

SELECTION AND IMAGINATION

EVEN assuming that through the medium of historical sources the historian can ascertain facts — I say facts and not *all* facts — and their relations, and that the social scientist is entitled to make use of those facts in order to ascertain laws, there still remain other difficulties which do not depend on the material with which we work, but on our minds.

Because of the mere fact that he investigates one group of events rather than another, the historian is obliged to exclude from his attention all the events having no bearing on those which interest him. The student of the history of a given country during a given period must neglect the history of all other countries and of the same country at all other periods. The student of economic history must put political history in the background; the student of intellectual history must do the same with political and economic history, and so on. Facts having fundamental importance for one historian may be ignored by another. This selecting of facts depends exclusively on the personal preferences of the historian. The historian amputates reality.

All this is true. But there is not a scientist who is not obliged to select as the subject of his research certain groups of facts, ignoring all others. No one can study everything. The only end to which a scientist can reasonably aspire is that of knowing only those facts which he sets out to investigate. The historian, no less than the scientist, in selecting one group of facts rather than another, makes a necessary abstraction and not an arbitrary mutilation.

At this point a fresh obstacle arises. What the past has left behind is always broken by more or less wide gaps. The historian has before him a jigsaw puzzle from which many pieces have disappeared. These gaps can be filled only by his imagination. Now, a work of imagination is not a scientific but an artistic work.

At the root of this argument lies the prejudice that the scientist never needs imagination. The truth is that the scientist does need imagination in his work. When facts and their correlations do not present a coherent picture, he has recourse to a hypothesis in order to fill gaps and overcome inconsistencies. All great scientific discoveries have been begotten of some bold hypothesis covering a vast domain of previously disconnected facts. That hypothesis was the fruit of a powerful imagination. Copernicus and Newton were men of gigantic imagination. From this point of view, it may be said that the great scientist is a great poet.

That does not imply that the imagination of the scientist is identical with that of the poet. In creating his characters and the milieu in which they have their being, the artist blends real facts with imaginary events, exactly as he chooses. Nobody would expect Shakespeare to produce Hamlet's birth certificate, or would investigate exactly how rotten was the state of Denmark in Hamlet's day. The artist is not even bound to give an air of probability to his imagined characters and situations. Caliban is outside all verisimilitude. Undoubtedly the artist is not entirely free to make his creations do as he pleases. However imaginary the characters and the conditions in which they are placed, they must act in accordance with an inner logic, analogous to that which might have been expected of them had they been men in real life. But when he makes his first assumption the artist is free to select and combine the data of experience according to the dictates of his own imagination.

The scientist finds himself in quite a different situation. After he has chosen his subject, the facts are there in front of him. He may not ignore a single one of them. A single fact which cannot be brought into line wrecks his hypothesis. Science is a work of imagination into which all proved facts must fit.

In art, reality is the handmaiden of imagination. In science, imagination is the handmaiden of reality. The artist is a creator. The scientist is a discoverer. Nobody calls Pasteur an artist or Shakespeare a scientist, though both possessed and made use of tremendous imaginative powers.

The scientist errs when a discrepancy arises between the description he gives of reality and reality itself. The failure of the artist arises from a disproportion between the emotions he seeks to arouse, the means he chooses to arouse them, and the results he actually achieves.

The imagination of the historian is like that of the scientist. The historian is strictly limited by the data furnished by his sources. He is not permitted freely to invent or combine events, their details, and the circumstances in which they took place. Only a Philistine expects the artist to give proofs of what his imagination has created, whereas any sensible man demands of the historian proofs and documents.

When an archaeologist states that the missing head of a statue must have worn a helmet, he is certainly working with the aid of his imagination. When he has achieved his demonstration his task is ended. It is outside his job to assert *without proof* that the missing head must have had a certain type of features rather than another, and that the helmet must have had a certain definite ornamentation rather than another. Still less has he the right to assert *without proof* that the statue formed part of a larger group, or to name *without proof* the other personages forming the group. If he ventures into the field of non-demonstrable hypothesis, his work loses historical value and becomes the arbitrary assertion of an ill-disciplined mind.

On the other hand, the sculptor who restores the statue by supplying the missing head has a certain amount of leeway in rendering the features of the head and the ornamentation of the helmet, even though he is not free to change the sex of the statue and although he is bound to respect the artistic style of the period to which the statue belongs. If the restoration of the statue were entrusted to another sculptor, equally scrupulous in respecting the fundamental data of the problem, he would nevertheless conceive the head in his own individual way. Now, in setting his creative faculty to work, the sculptor performs an artistic task similar to that of the literary biographer who invents dialogues, soliloquies, and speeches, more or less probable but not documentable. The sculptor might go still further and introduce the restored statue into a group of his own invention. In this case his work would be analogous to that of Alexandre Dumas writing *The Three Musketeers*. The archaeologist, being an historian, stops precisely at the point where the sculptor, being an artist, starts working.

If one has made clear to oneself the difference between artistic and scientific imagination, one does not run the risk of extolling intuition, inspiration, illumination, volcanic eruption, or whatever else one may wish to call the subconscious activities of the mind, as a source of knowledge superior to rational activities.

To be sure, hypotheses and discoveries are often born of sudden illuminations which are the outcome of a mysterious process taking place in the subconscious without any apparent contribution of logical reasoning. But after the illumination normal rational procedure has to come in. Only when the result of the illumination has been tested by such a procedure does it become a certainty. A scholar who announces that he has had an illumination and stops there, demanding that other scientists accept it without question, may be a genius, but he may also be a charlatan, or a crank. It is only through the normal procedure of logical reasoning that he can show that his intuition deserves acceptance. The historian or the social scientist cannot any more than any other scientist claim the right to withhold his credentials. Irrational ways may lead to the discovery of truth, but only by rational methods can truth be proved.

VII

BIAS AND HYPOTHESIS

VII

BIAS AND HYPOTHESIS

THERE is, however, a difference between history and the social sciences on the one hand and the physical sciences on the other.

Among the facts of the physical world there exists no link analogous to that purposiveness which, in human events, links effects to causes. The brick which by falling from a roof kills a man had no intention of killing its victim. Had the victim been killed by a fellow man, there would have been more than the mere death; there would have been the intention of killing. In human activities the cause is not only the indispensable antecedent but also the intention which produced the event. Where physical facts are concerned the scientist should speak of indispensable or conditioning antecedents and not of causes. The concept of cause is of anthropomorphic origin and should be made use of only when human phenomena are being investigated.

From this difference arises an essential divergence in the techniques of the scientist who deals with the physical world on the one hand, and of the historian and social scientist on the other. Where physical facts are concerned, the scientist is obliged to look at them from without. The historian and the social scientist can look at human facts not only from without but also from within. And in looking at them from within they are able to utilize the analogy between their own personal experience and that of the men who were the authors of the facts under investigation.

We reject the theory that the intellectual movement of the eighteenth century was the sole cause of the French Revolution because we know that there participated in that upheaval large masses of peasants and workers, illiterate masses lacking any knowledge of philosophical or political doctrines; and by analogy with our personal experience we hold that, were we illiterate and ignorant, and were we to revolt against the society in which we live, the cause of our revolutionary activities should be traced not to ideological impulses but to other causes — for instance, to our economic ills. On the other hand, we hold that among the causes of the French Revolution should also be numbered the philosophical and political doctrines developed in France during the half century preceding the Revolution, because we have noticed that the cultivated classes continually invoked such doctrines while they were destroying the old regime; and again the analogy with our personal experience leads us to think that none of us when taking part in a revolutionary movement would publicly profess philosophical and political doctrines which did not really form an ingredient in our beliefs.

All the reasonings of the historian and the social scientist can be reduced to this common denominator of analogy with our inward experience, whereas the scientist who is concerned with physical phenomena lacks the help of this analogy.

It follows that the broader the experience of the historian the better he will be able to understand the past. One who has a wide experience of economic facts will be more successful as an interpreter of the economic life of a thousand years ago than one who lacks all experience in that field. One who has a wide experience of military facts will be more successful in studies of military history than one whose training has been exclusively literary.

But precisely here lies one of the most insidious stumbling blocks for both history and the social sciences. The personal experience of one man is not necessarily the personal experience of another. Each one looks with different eyes at the events which he is trying to understand. Goethe remarked that history must be rewritten from time to time, not only because new facts have been discovered but above all because every generation comes forward with new interests and new ways of looking at things and consequently observes the past from different angles than theretofore.

These new standpoints are not always the outgrowth of objective observation. They are more often nothing but preconceptions and bias.

The historians of classical antiquity and of the Middle Ages believed in portents, and through them they explained victories, defeats, famine, and abundance. The writers of the eighteenth century did not believe in miracles. They regarded priests of all religions as imposters and explained miracles as the impostures of priests. Today we have a more profound knowledge of the normal and abnormal psychology of individuals and crowds. Therefore we do not regard as impostures all the miracles which the historical sources of antiquity and the Middle Ages report; instead we gather from this information invaluable data for studying the religious mentality and the psychology of the masses. For Bossuet, the story of the human race evolved according to a wise design of Providence. Voltaire made fun of preëstablished harmonies. Buckle explained the phases of civilization by the progress or decay of science. For Carlyle, the heroes are the makers of history. According to Marx, social, political, and even religious changes are reflections of the changing economic substructure. We can all think of instances of the perversions in historical writing caused by nationalistic passions and of the pernicious effect that history vitiated by nationalistic bias exerts upon the public mind. I sometimes think that, if peace is to be enforced on earth, most professors of history — at least in Europe — would have to be hanged.

Can the historian or the social scientist divest himself of his own prejudices? If not, what becomes of his so-called scientific knowledge?

Many historians and social scientists are haunted by the fear of being accused of bias. In order to avoid this danger they stifle their opinions as if they were unmentionable diseases and confine themselves to accumulating facts without any attempt at coördination. Since they say nothing, they run no risk of falling into error. But to avoid the risk of falling into error they give up the use of reason. On their dull and colorless books Pascal's formula may fittingly be placed: *Abêtissez-vous.*

Others, taking courage in both hands, set forth all the interpretations of which a given group of facts is capable and give *both sides,* as this procedure is commonly called. At this point they wash their hands of the matter like Pontius Pilate and leave the reader to answer for himself the question, "What is truth?" If they were dealing with the Dreyfus case, they would put before the reader all the arguments for or against Dreyfus' innocence and then they would say: "Be this as may, both sides thought they were right." They are like jurymen who think that in order to remain impartial they always should give open verdicts. Their "objectivity" is so punctilious that they would attain the consummation of felicity if they might be described as "inclining neither on the one hand to partiality nor on the other to impartiality."

Happy are the fanatics who are genuinely convinced of their impartiality and who tranquilly inject their biases into all their investigations and conclusions, holding that their biases are undisputed and indisputable truths. Pareto affords an amusing instance of the social scientist who is truly convinced that he is unbiased, serene, and detached, despite the fact that he is a most violently passionate man. His *Mind and Society* has been aptly described as the bitter invective of a disillusioned believer in liberalism, who can never mention democratic and humanitarian ideas without gibes and insults and calls for the man of force who kills humanitarians like noxious beasts. Yet he always feels sure that his hatred is the quintessence of scientific objectivity, and never harbors the least suspicion that it is the upshot of nonlogical preconceptions or, as he would say, of residues.

I, for my part, declare that my mind is carpeted with biases — religious, philosophical, scientific, social, political, national, and even personal — and that I constantly make use of my biases in my studies. I am not ashamed of this fact, because biases are not irreconcilable with scientific research.

The scientist must continually have recourse to hypotheses in order to find out facts and explain their correlations. His hypotheses are not always constructed as explanations of already known facts; they may also be anterior to any research. They may even have been suggested by irrational preconceptions or biases. Pasteur used to say that preconceptions are one of the greatest assets of the experimenter. They serve as guiding threads. A certain number are discarded as the search progresses; one fine day the scientist can prove that one of them covers all the facts requiring explanation. It is therefore no longer a hypothesis but a certainty. Duclaux, the most eminent of Pasteur's disciples, in his book *Pasteur: histoire d'un esprit* (Paris: Masson, 1896) has shown that some of the greatest discoveries of the master originated from erroneous assumptions.

When the scientist finds himself confronted with a maze of facts which he is unable at first trial to coördinate into a coherent system, he has recourse to the expedient *Divide et Impera* (Divide and Rule). He isolates one of the facts from the mass, assumes it to be the fundamental one, and tries to group the others around it. As he proceeds, he encounters a certain number of facts which are not amenable to his hypothesis. These facts he subjects to a similar process of grouping under another fact assumed to be fundamental. When a certain number of groups have thus been constituted, the problem arises of fitting all the groups together and thus building a single coherent system. If too many facts remain refractory, the scientist is driven to the conclusion that his initial hypotheses were unsound. He has to begin afresh the process of grouping single facts and coördinating groups into a new system according to different hypotheses, and he continues in this way until he achieves complete unification. For instance, the variations of climate are determined not only by differences of latitude but also by altitude, by distance from the sea, by the existence of hot or cold ocean currents, by a north or south exposure, etc. Physical geography traces each feature of a given climate to its cause and groups all causes into a hierarchical system under the fundamental factor of latitude.

When an historian or a social scientist is prompted by his bias to group facts into a system under which they are refractory, he is like the scientist who bases his unification on an arbitrary hypothesis. The bias at the start serves as a framework, however arbitrary, into which the facts may or may not be fitted. Fresh data, as they come to light, marshal themselves on one side or the other of the bias. A battle takes place between the two armies of proofs; the scholar follows the vicissitudes of the battle, searching for fresh data to buttress his preconceived ideas. However, he may discover only facts under the weight of which his preconception crumbles. Meanwhile, he has constructed a fresh hypothesis better fitted to the facts. Without the initial assumption the facts would have remained a meaningless jumble, and every added fact would have served only to make confusion worse confounded. In history and the social sciences, as well as in any other scientific search, preconceived ideas, no less than dispassionate hypotheses, fulfill a useful task.

It was the biased controversies between Catholics and Protestants from the sixteenth century onwards which gave impetus to the study of the origins of Christianity. Had there never been prejudices for or against the value of the Bible as an historical source, much of the work on Semitic languages and many archæological excavations in the Near East would never have been undertaken. Geological and biological studies have been prompted to a great extent by religious or irreligious, spiritualistic or materialistic biases. There are wrong but lucky biases by which every scientist would be happy to have been misled. The discovery of America was no doubt a happy event, for Europeans, if not for the natives. Christopher Columbus would never have ventured on his voyage had he not had in mind a correct hypothesis, that of the roundness of the earth, and two mistaken hypotheses, (1) that the radius of the earth was far smaller than it really is, and (2) that Asia extended eastward much farther than is actually the case. To these biases one has to add a perhaps arbitrary assumption — that God had chosen precisely Columbus to carry the Christian faith to peoples still in darkness — and, finally, a practical purpose, the desire for commercial gain.

Marx, in studying the economic history of England in the period of the industrial revolution, noticed that this revolution had been the result of the steam engine, and he formulated the law that all social changes, economic, political, legal, intellectual, moral, and religious, are the effect of changes in the technique of production. A broader examination of historical facts leads us to hold that innovations in the technique of production have undoubtedly always had social consequences that have been as marked as the innovation was important; but the innovations themselves were the outgrowth of intellectual exploration and often of chance, the causes of which cannot be traced to the economic substructure of society. On the other hand, social changes have not always been the result of innovations in methods of production. There is no proof that the military anarchy which disorganized the Roman Empire in the third century A.D., the rise and spread of Christianity, the barbarian conquests, were preceded by any innovation in the technique of production.

The law of Marx was the upshot of a false generalization, and behind that false generalization were his social biases. But this mistaken law gave rise to a vast body of studies on economic history. And from the facts so ascertained we have been led to the discovery of another law which can be formulated as follows: "Economic, social, political, and intellectual activities are interdependent; the structure of society cannot undergo a change in one of its parts without correlative changes in all the others." As a consequence, whoever today ignored economic events in explaining historical developments would be like a physiologist who ignored anatomy while studying the behavior of the human body. The influence of Marx has been tremendous even upon those historians who detest his political doctrines.

From the fact that Pareto is biased against humanitarian and democratic ideals, one is not entitled to draw the conclusion that his doctrines are wrong. His bias may have led him to discover truths which otherwise would have escaped him.

The critic of a book who believes his job well done when he has exposed the bias of the author and dismissed the book as biased shows that he is ignorant of the first elements of critical method. Any serious scholar knows full well that "the individual motives of a writer are altogether irrelevant in determining the logical force of his argument. . . . If the premises are sufficient, they are so no matter by whom stated. The personal history of Gauss is entirely irrelevant to the question of the adequacy of his proof that every equation has a root; and the inadequacy of Galileo's theory of the tides is independent of the personal motives which led Galileo to hold it." [1] To note the bias of a writer is useful — nay, more, necessary. But what matters is whether the writer has suppressed or distorted facts in order to indulge his bias. The critic must bring forward the facts suppressed or distorted and not merely dismiss the book because of its bias. The fact is that the critic would not dismiss the book were it permeated with the bias dear to his own heart. He would then extoll the author as unbiased, impartial, and broad-minded.

Doubtless preconceptions are dangerous. The historian or the social scientist who is not ready to cast them aside at need is apt to keep in the shade those facts which do not fit into his cherished scheme, and to give undue prominence to those which agree with his partisan spirit. But to withdraw from the historian or the social scientist the right to preconceptions and biases would be to dam up many fountainheads of precious discovery. On the other hand, the historian or the social scientist must be conscious that he is biased and must be on the

[1] M. R. Cohen and Ernest Nagel, *An Introduction to Logic and Scientific Method* (New York, 1934), p. 380.

watch against his bias. He should ask himself at every point of his investigation what objections might be raised by a well-informed person of opposite bias. Further, he should frankly confess his bias to the reader so that the reader, in turn, may be put on his guard. The difference between the historian and the propaganda agent does not consist in the fact that the former is not biased, while the latter is, or that the former states only facts which can be proved to be true, while the latter circulates false information. Both may make correct and incorrect statements. But the historian presents honestly to his public all the versions of a controversial fact which are known to him, and gives all the arguments which lead him not only to accept one version but to reject the others. The propaganda agent prefaces his statements with the boast that he is unbiased, impartial, and open-minded, and swears that he is telling the truth, the whole truth, and nothing but the truth, but he selects according to his own bias the facts which he is to expound and those which he is to conceal. And when he cannot conceal a version different from his own, he distorts the arguments which militate in its favor, and thus attempts to persuade his public to believe something they would not believe if they were given all the facts and arguments for or against his version. The propaganda agent is dishonest even when he has no need to lie, because it is his intention to deceive even when he is telling the truth. The historian, like any other honest scientist, may be led into error by his bias. Therefore his statements must be subjected to the same critical analysis as those of any other scientist. But, even when he errs, he remains an honest man and a scientist.

This, however, is not the whole story. Other factors must be taken into account.

VIII

UNIQUE AND RECURRING FACTS

VIII

UNIQUE AND RECURRING FACTS

IN the physical world we find, as a rule, phenomena with close similarities. Human events, on the contrary, are often endowed with so many individual features of their own that they can be identified with no other human event. A lion is similar to another lion. But what similarity can one find between the minds of Buddha, Caesar, and Shakespeare? One might as well seek similarities between a lamb, a tiger, and a nightingale. Even if one groups great men according to their fields of action — for instance, Buddha with Christ, Caesar with Napoleon, and Homer with Shakespeare — one cannot say that the two founders of world-wide religions, or the two army chiefs, or the two poets resemble each other in the same way that two lambs, two tigers, or two nightingales resemble each other.

Benedetto Croce, a contemporary philosopher whom I sometimes manage to understand, has deduced from this difference the thesis that history is not a science but an art. Adopting one of Schopenhauer's doctrines, he maintains that history, like art, is the description of individual facts, whereas science is the grouping of the individual under the general and the formulation of laws. The facts with which science deals are material facts and repeat themselves, while those which history deals with are spiritual and never recur. "The material of history," he writes, "is the singular in its singularity and contingency, that which is once and then is never again, the fleeting network of a human world which drifts like clouds before the wind and is often totally changed by unimportant events."

I submit that two objections may be raised against Schopenhauer's and Croce's theory:

1. Description of individual facts or objects is not art but the first stage of scientific work, the second stage being classification and construction of laws. Science is a process of ascension from the individual to the class. The botanist could not arrange plants according to genus and species without the preliminary work of describing each individual. Croce himself has to admit that artistic creation may correspond to no existing objects outside the imagination of the artist, while history has to conform to concrete reality. Thus, having catalogued

history under the heading of art, he is obliged to embark upon a fresh distinction to the effect that art represents the possible individual, whereas history represents the individual who has really existed.

2. The difference between material facts that are recurrent and spiritual facts that happen but once does not exist. The successive stages in the formation of the earth's crust have occurred once and have never occurred again. The destruction of the cities of Pompeii and of Herculaneum took place once and never took place again. These facts belong not to the spiritual world but to the material world. On the contrary, many spiritual facts do repeat themselves. Millions of men speak the same words, conforming to the same phonetic, morphological, and grammatical laws; they reason in the same way; they have the same religious dogmas; they build houses and cities; they buy and sell, marry, help one another, wage war, and so on. The history of economic, social, religious, moral, and intellectual life and of legal relationships consists of spiritual facts which recur in a form which remains unchanged or is slightly changed in a large number of individuals.

There is an equivocation in this word "recur."

One million dollars in my pocket and one million dollars in my mind are one million dollars. But they are not one and the same million dollars which recurs. They are different because they are located in different spots: one million is in my pocket and the other is in my mind. This is an essential difference. A million college boys going to school are not the same individual boy repeating himself a million times. They are a million different boys who behave in the same way. The logicians of the Middle Ages used to say: *Si duo sunt idem, non faciunt idem:* Two things, though identical, do not make one single thing. Two sheep do not make one sheep who recurs. When we say that two sheep are identical, we mean only that they have so many features in common that their individual features may be ignored. But any shepherd would raise his eyebrows if we told him that the sheep in his flock were identical, and he would think that we had gone out of our minds if we stated that all his sheep were a single sheep which recurs. His practiced eye knows how to distinguish one sheep from another, and his good sense tells him that each of his sheep is unique.

All facts in the spiritual as well as in the material world are unique. They occur once and never occur again. But there are facts that have nothing in common with other facts — for example, the geological formation of the earth — and of these facts we say that they do not recur; and there are facts which more or less resemble other facts — a lion that resembles all other lions, a person who goes to school like millions of other persons — and of these facts we say that they *repeat themselves.*

There is, however, at the root of Croce's theory an important element of truth: the scientist who studies the physical world often deals with facts which have in common a large number of features. Every year under a given climate, at the same season, the same flowers blossom and the same crops are ripe. Every day there is a sunrise and a sunset. Every moment men and animals are born and die. Of all these phenomena we say that they *recur.* In the world of human action, on the contrary, the events which have peculiar features of their own are the rule, and of them we say, therefore, that they *do not recur.* It is because of this diversity in the material with which they deal that the historian and the social scientist are severely handicapped in their work.

When the historian asks, let us say, whether submarine warfare was the decisive factor in bringing about the intervention of the United States in the World War, he poses a problem analogous to that which the physicist solves when he determines, for example, the cause or the causes of dew. The physicist observes, first of all, that dew is different from rain and from the moisture of fog. Then he observes that there are other cases of moisture analogous to dew: for instance, the moisture which bedews a cold metal when we breathe on it, or that which appears on the outside of a glass of water fresh from the well in hot weather, or on the inside of windows when rain or hail chills the external air. In comparing these cases, the scientist finds that they all contain the phenomenon which was proposed as the subject of the investigation, and all these instances agree in one respect: the coldness of the object bedewed in comparison to the air in contact with it. There is no need to follow the scientist to the end of this investigation. The entire process has been described in a classic page of John Stuart Mill's *System of Logic*. The important thing to note for our purpose is that the scientist could not make all his observations and

hypotheses if he had to deal only with the case
of dew and not with the many cases of dew,
rain, fog, moisture on cold metal, on glass or
on windows. Newton could advance his hypothesis of gravitation and reduce all the move-
ments of the heavenly bodies to one principle,
because each body through centuries had appeared to observers a great many times in different parts of the heavens and with constant
periodicity. Had each heavenly body appeared
only once and then disappeared for all time, it
would not have been possible either to determine any constant of its appearance or to formulate a law of those constants. A comet
which has appeared once, and then no more,
gives the astronomer no opportunity for any
conclusion.

The historian is often confronted with facts
that are unique. If there had been in history
not one but at least two World Wars like that
of 1914–1918, and if in one of them the German
Government had not embarked upon submarine warfare, and if without submarine warfare there had been no American intervention,
the difference would afford us the opportunity
of evaluating with certainty the part played in
1917 by submarine warfare, and the problem

would be solved in the sense that in 1917 submarine warfare was the decisive factor. Failing this opportunity, we investigate the entrance of the United States into the World War under the same conditions as an astronomer when dealing with a comet that has appeared once and has not reappeared, or as a physicist trying to ascertain the cause of dew, knowing only one case of dew.

When the historian or social scientist deals with a large number of facts more or less resembling one another, the so-called recurrent facts — as for example, words of the same language, economic activities, legal transactions, popular superstitions — his position is comparatively good. The deciphering of an Egyptian or Assyrian text is as certain as the forecasting of an eclipse: every time we meet with a given sign, we are sure of meeting with a given idea. This comes about because the historical sources present the same sign for the same idea not once but many times and in different combinations with other signs, and it is by comparing the different cases in which the same sign appears that the scholar can ascertain its meaning. The legal and moral relations between father and children in the Roman world are known to us with reasonable certainty, at least in their normal aspects, because historical sources yield information on a large number of Roman families resembling one another.

These opportunities, however, are offered us only in respect to the elementary facts of human life, in so far as all men in a given society at a given period of history speak in the same way, treat their wives and children in the same manner, have the same religious beliefs, engage in the same economic dealings. But as the similarities between facts become fewer and the differences multiply, the difficulties of analyzing and classifying them increase.

IX

COMPLEXITY, MEASUREMENT, AND EXPERIMENT

COMPLEXITY, MEASUREMENT, AND EXPERIMENT

NOT only do the historian and the social scientist deal with phenomena which are often unique, but their phenomena often form voluminous and complex tangles.

The more numerous the pieces of a puzzle, the more difficult it is to fit them together. The more complex the tangle of facts, the more difficult to arrange them in a sequence of cause and effect, and to classify them according to constant similarities or differences. It was more difficult for Newton to work out the hypothesis of gravitation than for a chemist of today to determine the reactions of a given body when it is placed in contact with other bodies. In the spiritual world, also, the simpler the phenomena, the more the work of the historian and the social scientist approximates to the type of the exact sciences. Some branches of historical studies — for instance, paleography, numismatics, diplomatics — have reached a high degree of certainty owing to the fact that they ignore all historical events but one, whether it be writing, coins, or juridical formulas. Glottology, or the science of language, deals with words and groups of words, that is to say, facts which are not as intricate as many others; this is one of the reasons why in classifying languages and establishing the laws of each language or group of languages glottology has attained a marvelous certainty of results and can bear comparison with the most accredited of the exact sciences. By separating economic facts from other social facts, the economists have been able to formulate economic laws which have all the characteristics of certainty; for instance, if there is inflation of currency, prices soar.

But the more complex events become, the more our difficulties increase. The intervention of the United States in the World War was undoubtedly caused by the concurrence of many factors: pressure on the part of bankers who had been intermediaries in loans of American money to England and France, and of investors who had put their money into these loans; counter-pressure from other bankers favorable to Germany and from investors in German securities; pro-Entente propaganda, which found an indulgent hearing among Protestants, the liberal-minded middle classes, and citizens of Anglo-Saxon origin; pro-German counter-propaganda, which was readily accepted by citizens of German and Irish origin and by Roman Catholics; pacifist propaganda and revolutionary propaganda à la Lenin, which, for motives quite different from pro-German propaganda, tried to keep the country out of war; the blunders of German diplomacy; submarine warfare; the preconceptions, worries, hopes, and delusions of Wilson, his intimate advisers, and the other leaders of American public opinion; and perhaps other factors of which I am not aware. It is not an easy task to assign to each of these factors its appropriate place in an all-inclusive system of causes and effects.

When investigating a tangle of factors in the physical world, the scientist is, as a rule, able to measure them; that is, he can ascertain their dimensions, weight, and duration in time. The physicist can determine the proportion to which each of the operative forces has contributed to bring about a given result; the chemist can determine how many atoms of hydrogen and oxygen produce a molecule of water; the astronomer can measure the distance between the stars, their velocity, their rises, and so on. The French mathematician and astronomer, Laplace, could conceive of a mind able to forecast the movement of all celestial bodies for the whole of the future, provided it were given all the masses, with their positions and their initial velocity. The social scientist might also forecast the behavior of all the men and women who compose a society provided he knew with certainty the internal mechanism of all the men and women who make up that society. But he does not know with certainty even his own internal mechanism. He has, as a rule, no objective standard by which to measure the importance of facts.

The historian is in the position of a geographer who is called upon to describe a mountain chain without instruments with which to measure its length and breadth, the altitude of its peaks, and the depths of its valleys. In addition, the historian cannot even inspect the chain personally because the chain has disappeared, and he has to be content with descriptions made by people who saw it but did not take measurements.

Social scientists rely on statistics. Statistics —

when not faked — supply a means of measuring the dimensions of certain social phenomena: births, marriages, deaths, imports, exports, revenue from taxation, crime, school attendance, and so forth. But the systematic assembling of statistical data was begun only during the last century, and even today there are happy countries without statistical bureaus. Moreover, the statistical method does not work when one passes from more simple to more complex phenomena. Think of the difficulty one has in grading a boy's examination paper if that paper is on the border line between pass and fail — as most papers are. Yet the grading of an examination paper is a comparatively simple problem of measurement.

Was submarine warfare the decisive factor in bringing about America's entrance into the World War? To answer this question we should be in a position to measure the strength of each current which contributed to that result, and to draw a graph showing how each force combined with the others. This cannot be done. Therefore the controversy to determine the decisive factor will never end. Perhaps President Wilson himself would have been unable to solve the problem satisfactorily.

In October 1938 a heated controversy broke out in London between the Soviet Ambassador to Great Britain and Lord Winterton, a member of the British Government. Lord Winterton stated that during the Czechoslovakia crisis Russia had offered only "vague promises" to Czechoslovakia. The Soviet Ambassador to Great Britain called upon the British Foreign Minister and protested that Lord Winterton's statement was a "complete perversion of the actual position of the USSR," which had been "explicit and did not leave room for misunderstanding." Lord Winterton again insisted that "Russia did not make any precise promise of military assistance." Which of these two gentlemen was lying? To solve this problem with certainty, one would need an objective standard in order to measure when promises made by diplomats are still "vague" and "leave room for misunderstanding," and at what point they become "explicit" and "precise"; moreover, assuming that such a standard were available, it would also be necessary to measure by another objective standard whether the diplomat who has to decide whether a promise is "vague" or "explicit" is willing to decide one way or another. A few weeks later another controversy arose between the President of the Bar Association of the City of New York and the President of the Federal Bar Association of New York, New Jersey, and Connecticut. The former maintained that a law he did not like had been hurriedly enacted. The latter maintained that nobody could "even attempt" to utter the charge that the law had been hurriedly pushed through Congress.[1] The lawyer who did not like the law would have maintained that the law had been hurriedly pushed through even if it had had behind it not one year but decades of preparation; and the other would have been of the opinion that the law was the result of mature deliberation even if it had been introduced not one year but one day before it was passed in its final form. The whole argument hinges on the meaning of the word "hurriedly," and there is no objective standard which might permit us to decide what we mean exactly by the word "hurriedly."

A social scientist of our day has brought before a tribunal of his own devising a crowd of luckless men who handed down their thoughts to posterity between the years 560 B.C. and 1920 A.D., and has assigned to each a value on a scale

[1] *New York Times*, Nov. 4, 1938.

ranging from 1 to 12. Socrates is rated 9, Plato 12, Aristotle 12, Thomas Aquinas 12, Leonardo da Vinci 8, Leibnitz 9, Kant 12. I myself should rate Socrates and Leonardo da Vinci 12, Aristotle 10, Plato 9, Leibnitz and Kant 8, and St. Thomas Aquinas 7. A third might rate them still differently, and each one would be right, according to his own lights. Dante is rated 8, together with Shakespeare and Schiller. I have no quarrel with Schiller, but I fear that Dante and Shakespeare might not get on with him. As regards many writers of antiquity there is a great freedom of judgment, since their works are wholly or practically lost. Doubts multiply when we examine the categories under which these schoolboys are classified. Dante is to be found neither under the heading of *mysticism,* nor *fideism,* nor *ethics of love,* but under that of *equilibrium of temporalism and eternalism,* together with Schiller and Fichte, and, again, he goes hand in hand with Aristotle and Epicurus under *determinism.* Petrarch falls under the heading of *ethic of principles,* on a par with Savonarola, who was roasted on account of his principles, and with Calvin who roasted Servetus, again on account of principles, whereas Petrarch never thought of roasting anybody, much less of being roasted, on account of his principles.

Again, by what objective standards can one rate the gravity of revolutionary upheavals? The social scientist mentioned above rates the English Revolution of the seventeenth century with 77.27; the French Revolution of 1789–99 with 79.43; the Paris Commune of 1871 with 21.53; the collapse of the Bismarckian Empire in 1918 with 36.73; the Russian Revolution of 1917–21 with 63.08, and so on. I am not a social scientist but a mere historian, and as such I view with sorrow the tremendous amount of ingenuity and time wasted to determine that between the gravity of the French Revolution and that of the Bolshevist Revolution there exists the same reference as between 77.27 and 63.08. The only lesson to be gained from so many statistics is that the statistical method is valid when one wants to know the average weight of pigs of various ages but does not work when one wishes to measure the powers of the human brain or the strength of revolutions.

The historian has at his disposal only one objective standard — chronology. But order in time does not in itself establish a relationship of cause and effect. Not all events preceding another event stand in a causal relation to it. Chronology affords a negative rather than a positive help. It prevents us from substituting the effect for the cause, since a fact which is subsequent to another fact cannot have been the cause of that fact. But its usefulness ends there.

The woes of the historian and the social scientist are not yet told to an end.

When the scientist who deals with the physical world thinks he has detected a conditioning link between two or more phenomena, he resorts to experiment to verify his hypothesis; that is to say, he artificially reproduces those phenomena again and again, arranging them in different ways among themselves and in conjunction with other phenomena, to see whether the presence or the absence of the assumed cause is always followed by the presence or absence of the assumed effect. When he is wrong, his hypothesis is wrecked by his experiments or those of other scientists. Experiment is the surest instrument at the disposal of the investigator in the physical sciences. The advances made by the sciences from Galileo on are mainly due to the experimental method.

Whenever it is possible to apply the test of experiment, our minds are led toward a result which is, as Peirce says, *predestined,* and against which our preconceptions, our whims, our perversities, are powerless. The truth proved experimentally imposes itself upon us as does fate. We cannot oppose it.

The historian and the social scientist cannot apply to their hypotheses the supreme test of experiment. The best way of solving the problem of whether German submarine warfare was the decisive factor in bringing about American intervention in the World War would be to return to the years from 1914 to 1918, prevent the German Government from inaugurating submarine warfare, and then wait and see what develops. This we cannot do.

Under such conditions, bias has freer play in history and the social sciences than in the sciences of the physical world. Let us take the example of the social scientist who is trying to determine the laws of revolution. He must base his work on that of historians. But the Protestant Revolution is described by Catholic historians as well as by Protestant historians, the French Revolution by Monarchist and Republican historians, the Russian Revolution by

Bolshevists and White Russians. On which works must the social scientist base himself? If each one bases himself on the works which best suit his preconceptions, we shall then have not only divergent versions for each one of the different revolutions but also diverse laws for revolutions. Were we able to resort to experiment, the erroneous versions and the imaginary laws would be disproved, leaving only those hypotheses which are based on material not subject to doubt.

When one man says: "*If* the German Government had not started the submarine war, the intervention of the United States in the World War would never have taken place," and another man retorts: "Even *if* the submarine war had never been started, the United States would have entered the World War just the same," both make an experiment in their minds; that is, both reproduce in their minds the events of 1914 to 1918; then they do without one of them — the submarine war — after which they observe what results follow the omission. In the same way behave those who maintain that Hitler would not have dared go to war over the Sudeten Germans in September 1938, *if* the British Prime Minister had, from the beginning of the crisis, made it clear that he would not paralyze the French Government but stand by it, and those who maintain that *if* the British Prime Minister had taken this course the whole of Europe would have been plunged into war. Unfortunately, experiments made in our minds give different results according to the different minds in which they take place. Those who argue on the grounds of *ifs* are like a physicist who carries on experiments on magnetism in a room made of steel and disturbed by electrical waves. With *ifs* one can prove anything.

To be sure, not all of the physical sciences can resort to experiment. Newton did not demonstrate by experiments his hypothesis on gravitation. But he was dealing with phenomena which recur, can be measured, and had been observed through centuries. Very seldom do the historian and the social scientist possess such groundwork for their investigations.

To make up so far as possible for this drawback there is no other way than to create an environment of free competition between opposite biases. If he is pigheaded, the historian or the social scientist will overlook the facts which do not fit into his system and will continue to cling to his bias. But then another historian or another social scientist, animated by a different bias, brings to the fore the facts which his predecessor has ignored, and forms another picture, which may perhaps be no less distorted but at least reveals the possibility of another coördination. Then a third scholar comes along who, in that particular question, is free from bias. He checks the work of his predecessors, corrects distortions, fills the gaps, and welds all the fragments into a comprehensive and coherent system. Thus the veils are lifted one by one from the face of truth, and history and the social sciences achieve a greater measure of objectivity. This objectivity results not from the absence of bias but from controversy between conflicting preconceptions, a controversy which is at bottom coöperation. The scientist is not one who, wishing to open a door, must once and for all choose from among a bunch of keys the one key which alone is good. Scientific research is a series of successive approaches to truth, comparable to an exploration in an unknown land. Each explorer checks and adds to the findings of his predecessors, and facilitates for his successors the attainment of the goal they all have in common.

This is why history and the social sciences, more than any of the physical sciences, need an atmosphere of free competition between different schools of thought, in which all hypotheses and all proconceptions can be pitted one against the other. If liberty is suppressed in favor of a single school, it is the death warrant of our studies. The scholars of the dominant school, no longer stimulated by free competition, lose their capacity to renew their vitality, become mummified by the very monopoly they enjoy, and lapse into lazy repetition of official propaganda. If they do not demand free competition not only for themselves but for their rivals as well, the historian and the social scientist, more than any other scholars, accept both moral and intellectual degradation.

However, even in an atmosphere of intellectual liberty and free competition between different schools of thought, doubt and controversy are bound to be the lot of the historian and the social scientist.

X
PREVISION

X

PREVISION

IN dealing with phenomena which are recurrent, measurable, and not unduly complicated — and especially if hypotheses can be
subjected to the test of experiment — the investigator of the physical world can often fore-
tell with certainty that a given phenomenon
will be followed by another given phenomenon. Very seldom do human events permit
unerring forecasts of future recurrences.

A physician who is also a competent historian, Dr. Pieraccini, reconstructed by twenty
years of painstaking research the medical history of the famous Italian dynasty of the
Medici from the middle of the fourteenth century to its extinction in 1743, that is to say, over
four hundred years and through twelve generations. He examined the lives of one hundred
and twenty-one individuals, both male and fe-
male, having at his disposal letters, portraits,
even the reports of the physicians who attended
them during illness, and a wealth of other
manuscript and printed information. As far

as I know, no better historical contribution has ever been made to genetics. Yet let us suppose that Dr. Pieraccini, with the vast knowledge he has of the history of the Medici family, had been present at the birth of the last male of the family. Would he have been able to forecast that this child would die without issue and be the dullest and most insignificant offspring of a family which had produced so many first-rate men? No. Why? Because the factors which contribute toward building up the personality of a man are so numerous, and their interlocking is so complex, that nobody can know whether a newborn baby will be a man of genius or an idiot, a saint or a gangster, a football player or a weakling. His future is unpredictable.

Hegel wrote in his *Philosophy of History:* "The enterprise consisting in joining the Mediterranean with the Arabian Gulf and the Ocean is not so useful as one might be tempted to believe, for the Red Sea is not only difficult to navigate but also is swept during about nine months of the year by an incessant north wind, so that voyages from south to north are possible only during three months of the year." When the advisability of establishing railways was being discussed by the French House of Peers, the great mathematician Arago sided against railways, using as one of his arguments the great increase they would bring about in cases of colds and pneumonia. Economists have not yet succeeded in solving the problem of forecasting economic depressions; and, if a depression could be forecast, everybody would take the necessary measures to avoid it, so that in consequence the depression would not occur and the forecast would thus miscarry. In 1931 an American journalist took a fancy to gather a rich harvest of predictions which had been made from 1928 to 1931 by American "experts" on the prosperity which certainly awaited the United States.[1] Politicians, high federal officials, stock exchange presidents, leading bankers, big manufacturers, chairmen of railway and telephone companies and of associations of business men and farmers, professors of economics in universities, accredited writers on economics, lords of the press — none of them had the least suspicion that they were in the midst of the most terrific hurricane recorded in economic history.

Dr. A. Lawrence Lowell, President Emeritus

[1] A. Angly, *Oh Yeah?* (New York, 1931).

of Harvard University, has written an article in *The Harvard Guardian* in which he demands greater° foresight in foreign affairs on the part of responsible statesmen, and holds up to statesmen as models the military chiefs, "who are constantly studying the future, laying plans and changing them to meet improvements in weapons." I would not deny the necessity of foresight in all kinds of human affairs. Unfortunately, the foresight of military chiefs is no greater than that of civilian politicians. When a war occurs, one of two participants has to be the loser, that is, must have had insufficient foresight. Thus at least fifty per cent of military chiefs are no luckier than civilian politicians in their forecasts. During the World War there was not a single forecast by any military chief in any country which did not go wrong, including the forecast of that teacher of military science at the school for officers in Modena, Italy, who in August 1915, a year after the outbreak of the World War, was teaching his pupils that under modern economic conditions a war could not last more than four months. Now that the work of the chiefs who commanded the armies on all sides is becoming known, we can measure the intellectual

and moral poverty of those famous men, hide-
bound by routine, jealous of one another, and
more ready to sacrifice thousands of human
lives than to adopt a plan the success of which
might be credited to others. In all the documents now being published it is not the military chiefs who make the best showing but
politicians who many a time foresaw the dis-
asters brought on by the crass obstinacy of the
military chiefs, sought to retrieve their blunders, and bore the blame for those blunders in
the public eye rather than destroy the confidence of the public in their military leaders. It
is most likely that Tolstoy is right when he
maintains in his great novel *War and Peace*
that during a battle none of the military leaders understands what is happening until suddenly one side realizes that it has lost and, as a
consequence, the other side that it has won.

Moltke — the German army chief of 1866
and 1870, and not that of 1914 — used to say
that no army chief can foresee all that can happen during a campaign, nor can he be sure of
victory. He must choose a plan which, to his
mind, offers the maximum number of advan-
tages and the minimum number of dangers,
and then apply it resolutely, snatching every

advantage and making the best of its defects, ready to abandon it should a new plan occur to his mind which another summary calculation makes him think preferable to the first. All this is summed up in the statement that an army chief must be a very able man — which is rarely the case. At this point the "factory of fog" would start working and, since "art" is a kind of wastebasket into which everything which is not strict science is thrown, we should be told that, because great ability cannot be acquired by scientific devices, the army chief also is an "artist." The statement would be correct only if the word "art" in this connection acquired a meaning wholly different from that which is coupled with it when we say that a poem is a work of art. The artistic gifts of the poet are quite apart from those which are needed when a practical problem has to be faced. In this case "art" means quick observation, bold initiative, dogged perserverance, willingness to gamble, and other turns of mind which have nothing to do with either scientific or aesthetic definitions. They fall under the Aristotelian category of practical activities.

We are surrounded by innumerable seeds of possible events. Some seeds will develop; most

will lie sterile. We usually say that this is the
result of chance. But all that happens is the
necessary consequence of indispensable antecedents which, in their turn, are consequences
of other indispensable antecedents. We are
accustomed to apply the term "chance" not to
what might not have happened but to what we
should have been unable to forecast before it
happened. Chance is the unpredictable concurrence of unpredictable causal sequences.
When the unpredictable does happen, we then
realize that everything has taken place in an
unbroken line of cause and effect. The French
critic Sainte-Beuve wrote in his *Cahiers* in
April 1848, as he reflected upon what had happened in France in the preceding February:
"There is an infinite number of ways in which
a thing that is in process of happening may
materialize. When it has happened, people see
only one way. What we saw last February is a
fine case in point. The thing might have
turned out in many different ways. In fifty
years people will maintain that the way in
which it did turn out was a necessity." Thus
it is only the past that the historian and the
social scientist are able to predict with assurance. When we try to forecast the future we

estimate probabilities; we do not weigh certainties. Our forecasts are guesses and often mere gambles. When they prove correct, we are proud of our intelligence. When they go wrong, we forget them. Dreams also sometimes prove prophetic. Yet dreams are not scientific operations.

In October 1938 the Mayor of New York expressed the hope that "some day some one will hit upon the idea of a laboratory for government, where proper men and women may be trained for the responsibility of government, where we can abandon the hit-and-run system and take up government as a science, as it should be. Progress in mechanics, in electricity, in transportation, in chemistry, has gone so far ahead of government as to create the conditions under which we are now suffering." [2] A few days later, a father who was worried about the future of his three-year-old child if war were not abolished before his child came of age demanded that the disease of war be studied with the scientific methods used by medicine in attacking the germs producing other diseases: "What are the real causative agents of war? Where do they hide, these

[2] *New York Herald Tribune,* Oct. 30, 1938.

germs? How do they breed? What do they
thrive on? What are their media of existence?
Where are the points of infection? How is this
plague of war spread? Gigantic strides have
been made by research in medicine. If we were
to apply the methods of medicine and form a
research body to study the causes of war, our
approach to battle would be a more effective
one." [3] Then the President of Columbia University came to the fore and pronounced that
"If a world confronted by chaos and seemingly
insoluble problems is to survive and to go on to
new roads of progress, the scientific method
must be applied in studying and in solving
the political and economic enigmas ahead of
us." [4]

Alas! I very much fear that such hopes will
never be fulfilled. Mechanics, electricity, transportation, chemistry, medicine deal with physical phenomena, whereas government and war
are human phenomena, which can neither be
simplified, nor measured, nor experimented
upon. No laboratory for government, no scientific approach to battle against the microbe
of war can supply us with the foresight of

[3] *New York Herald Tribune*, Nov. 5, 1938.
[4] *New York Times*, Dec. 29, 1938.

future events, and thus we shall never be able to avoid miscalculations and blunders.

It is often asserted that we should feel a sense of responsibility toward the generations to come. But what do the teachers of this noble doctrine know about the ways of living, the ideals, the tastes of those infinite generations which are still to come? What must we do to content them? Not possessing the gifts of prophecy, we must be satisfied with asking ourselves what we would have wished our fathers and mothers to do to make us better and happier, and what we can do to make happier and better the men and women of our generation — at the most those of the next generation. Yet when I ask myself such questions I find it very difficult to give a sure answer to them. Usually the answer is suggested to me not by scientific foresight but by moral impulses from which I cannot separate myself; for were they to disappear from my make-up, my whole personality would disintegrate. And my answers are as old as the world: they can all be summed up in the old maxim of Christ that we should do unto others what we should like others to do unto us. For example, it would be a good thing for the generations to come if we did not increase the public debt for the purpose of satisfying our immediate needs. It is not necessary, however, to have studied much history or to have delved deeply into the social sciences to arrive at such an obvious conclusion.

XI
EXACT AND INEXACT SCIENCES

EXACT AND INEXACT SCIENCES

IF the historian and the social scientist have to deal with facts which are both unique and complex; if they are unable in most cases to measure their phenomena by objective standards; if they cannot apply to hypotheses the supreme test of experiment; if their forecasts are guesses and not prophecies; and if they cannot give sure prescriptions for social diseases — what then is history, what then are the social sciences? Are they sciences?

Many answer this question by stating that, since the historian and the social scientist are often unable to give their problems an indisputable solution, history and the social sciences are not sciences but branches of art. This is equivalent to considering art an unsuccessful science. An imperfect piece of scientific research would turn into a work of art. The investigator who failed to solve a problem would become a Byron or a Victor Hugo. The absurdity of such an implication is patent. Art is not a rudimentary science.

The true answer is forthcoming if one bears in mind that at the root of all the arguments which we have discussed until now lies the misconception that scientists know everything, are never beset by doubts or harried by disputes, always follow the rule of what Taine called *la raison raisonnante* — reasoning reason —, never feel the need of relying upon hypothesis or imagination, are immune from preconceptions and biases, can measure their phenomena and experiment. As a matter of fact, "scientists are human" whether they deal with the phenomena of the physical world or with those of human societies. Even among the physical sciences there exist domains which are not immune from doubts and controversies. At the core of each science lies a zone of firmly established facts; this zone is surrounded by an area of doubtful hypotheses, which is in its turn encircled by a *terra incognita*. The difference between one science and another and between two branches of the same science is not the difference between a "yes" and a "no" but that between a "more" and a "less." The more material phenomena gain in complexity and the less the scientists of the physical world can subject them to the test of experiment, the less

often can they make sure forecasts. When they
formulate a law, they always prudently affix to
it the qualification, "all other circumstances
remaining unchanged"; that is to say, if the
real phenomenon chanced to become part of a
more complex nexus of phenomena, some un-
predicted factor might upset all calculations,
the law might not work, and the forecast might
break down.

Meteorology is undoubtedly a science. But
meteorologists can forecast only tomorrow's
weather, or at most that of the day after tomorrow. They are often at a loss even over
tomorrow's weather and consequently put in
their bulletins "unsettled." This formula does
not mean that the weather is unsettled, but that
their ideas about it are. The hurricane which
swept New England in September 1938 was
not foreseen; the meteorologists had not even
said that the weather was unsettled.

In history and the social sciences the doubtful spots are far more numerous than in the
physical sciences. History and the social sciences fall under that category to which John
Stuart Mill applies the term "imperfect sciences." "There are reasons enough," he writes,
"why the moral sciences must remain inferior

to at least the more perfect of the physical; why the laws of their more complicated phenomena cannot be so completely deciphered, nor the phenomena predicted with the same degree of assurance. But though we cannot attain to so many truths, there is no reason that those we can attain should deserve less reliance or have less of a scientific character. . . . And this is what is or what ought to be meant by those who speak of sciences which are not *exact* sciences. . . . The science of human nature is of this description. It falls far short of the standard of exactness now realized in Astronomy; but there is no reason that it should not be as much a science . . . as astronomy was when its calculations had only mastered the main phenomena, but not the perturbations." Historians and social scientists are scientists, but with a small *s*. In comparison with those who deal with the physical world they are the poor relations among scientists. But even poor relations may be of use. Inexact sciences can be of service. A hatchet is not an instrument of precision, but it renders useful services, especially when wielded by a knowing hand.

We shall never be able to define by a mathematical coefficient the part played by submarine warfare in provoking the intervention of the United States in the World War. But one fact is certain: the intervention of the United States in the war occurred after the inauguration of submarine warfare. Moreover, we know that President Wilson, notwithstanding the fact that personal preconceptions drove him to side with England, notwithstanding the fact that several of his intimate advisers were in favor of England, never thought of intervention until after the beginning of submarine warfare. In fact, his presidential campaign in 1916 was based on the slogan: "He kept us out of war." Besides, when he did declare war, the United States was unprepared for immediate intervention despite the fact that the war had already been raging for two and a half years. From this data we are led to conclude that it was submarine warfare which led President Wilson to join the anti-German Entente. But there exists another fact. The inauguration of submarine warfare was followed not by the declaration of war on Germany but merely by the severance of diplomatic relations. War was declared only after the fall of the Czarist regime in Russia. Consequently, this event also contributed to the intervention of the United States in the war. It is impossible to assign to each cause of American intervention a numerical coefficient, and all our conclusions are bound to be only approximative. But there is no reason for condemning them as devoid of any foundation.

To be sure, the old doctrine that history is *magistra vitae* is an oversimplification. It has its antithesis in the doctrine that history only teaches that no one has ever learned from history. If Napoleon had asked Hannibal or Alexander the Great or Caesar what he was to do during his campaigns, it is quite probable that his predecessors would have had nothing to tell him, because the conditions under which their military operations were carried out were completely different from conditions in the time of Napoleon. It is impossible to deduce conclusions from facts which do not recur. Yet all army officers study the military experiences of their predecessors. Why? Because by acquainting themselves with the conditions in which their predecessors had to act, by perceiving why they acted as they did and not otherwise, and by scrutinizing the outcome of those actions, the army chief trains his mind, not to act in the same way but to be alert for all the elements of the new situation in which he himself will have to act, thus calculating all the eventualities and facing the unpredictable with greater wealth of experience.

At bottom, proverbs are formulations of imperfect laws suggested by experience. It would be a mistake to rely blindly on proverbs, especially when two proverbs stand in flat contradiction to each other. But neither would it be wise to ignore them completely, on the ground that they do not furnish us with infallible rules. The laws which the social sciences seek to define do not differ essentially from proverbs. They are proverbs worked out with greater discrimination — that is to say, founded on experiences which have been more carefully ascertained. This is the task of all sciences: to prolong and bring to a higher degree of exactitude and certitude the experiences of the common man.

The social scientist who studies economic phenomena will tell you that, all other conditions remaining equal, currency inflation will produce a rise in prices. The politician may resort to currency inflation either in order to meet some situation which without that measure would become intolerable, or in order to satisfy some sectional interests which mean to exploit inflation. If he knows nothing of that economic law, he will inflate the currency without taking the measures necessary to counteract the economic and social consequences of inflation. If he knows that economic law, he will know beforehand what consequences his policy will entail and will take precautionary measures to mitigate the inconveniences.

In 1896, in a work which has recently been translated into English by Arthur Livingston under the title *The Ruling Class,* an Italian social scientist, Gaetano Mosca, on the strength of wide and solid historical studies, formulated the following law: "In all societies, no matter how organized, even in those societies that are termed democracies, the government is controlled by an organized minority of the population." To this organized minority Mosca gave the name of "political class." Pareto reached an analogous conclusion but spoke of "élites," a rather misleading term which may suggest the notion of a natural superiority. If I am not mistaken, all historical knowledge corroborates Mosca's law. Any historian who analyzes the political constitution and events of a particular country at a given time, even if he does not know the law formulated by Mosca,

may — I venture to say, must — arrive at the
conclusion that, in that particular country, at
that given time, the government was controlled
by an organized minority; but this realization
would remain in his mind as an isolated fact,
and he would have arrived at it without any
other guide than his understanding. He may
even be led astray by some wrong hypothesis
or preconception which he might have avoided,
had he known Mosca's law. Knowing this
law, he not only possesses a guiding thread to
the understanding and interpretation of facts,
but he also finds that fresh facts confirm that
law. Moreover, after he has found that an
organized minority controls the rest of the
population, the historian will tackle many ac-
cessory problems with greater assurance. From
what social classes do the individuals come
who constitute the governing minority? How
are they selected? What are their rights and
duties with respect to the governed population? The origins, the method of selection, the
rights and duties of the political classes in
democratic countries like France, Great Britain,
and the United States, are different from those
of totalitarian countries like Russia, Italy, and
Germany. They differ in the various demo-

cratic countries as in the various dictatorial countries. If the historian had not been aided by Mosca's law in solving the fundamental problem, he might have come to wrong conclusions even about the secondary problems. In regard to a dictatorial regime, he might believe that the government is carried on not by a minority surrounding the dictator but by the dictator alone; or, as regards a democratic regime, he might conclude that the government is in the hands not of a minority of permanent officials and politicians accepted by the majority of the electorate but of the whole people.

There is need of many more historians who keep before their minds the laws formulated by social scientists, use them as working hypotheses in their work, and seek to discover whether or not such hypotheses are borne out by historical facts. And there is need of many more social scientists who realize the necessity of basing their work on facts carefully and critically ascertained, and not on information picked up at random from sources to which no historian worthy of the name would give the slightest degree of credence. A systematic cooperation between the historian and the social scientist would prove invaluable to both, if each, in his own field, wished to obtain less conjectural and more reliable results. History can contribute to the social sciences a foundation of carefully ascertained facts, and from them in turn it can obtain laws and hypotheses leading to a surer critical treatment and co-ordination of facts.

But even if this coöperation does become more general and systematic we must not entertain the illusion that we shall ever attain the precision and certainty which may be attained in many fields by the physical sciences — not, at least, until some genius invents instruments to measure the products of the human mind and to experiment on human societies as can now be done with guinea pigs.

XII
FROM HUMILITY TO TOLERANCE

XII

FROM HUMILITY TO TOLERANCE

FROM the fact that the sciences of the human world are unable to attain a degree of exactitude equal to that of the sciences of the physical world one conclusion must be drawn which is as certain as any of those which we have called predestined truths. This conclusion is that no one is infallible when forecasting the future of social life and undertaking the direction of it.

Any one of us, going out on the street, may be knocked down by an automobile, and this event is unpredictable. But this is a rather simple event, and the probabilities of avoiding an unpredictable of that type are so numerous in comparison with the contrary probabilities that it would be folly to remain eternally shut up to avoid the danger of being knocked down on going out. When the majority of American citizens adopted the principle of prohibition, they were wrong in forecasting the results of that constitutional amendment. A law like prohibition, promoted with the highest moral intentions, may produce wholly unsatisfactory results, especially from the moral standpoint. On the other hand, a banking law promoted by men concerned only with their own profit at the expense of the country at large may end by producing results beneficial to the country. No one can tell in advance with certainty what repercussions a change in American tariff or currency practices will have on the rest of the world or upon the United States itself. The art of government is to a large extent a gamble, precisely because the prevision of social facts is to a large extent a gamble.

Since no one is infallible in coping with social problems, the only way of tackling them lies in trying out various solutions one after the other. By trial and error — "muddling through," as the English say — a way out is found.

The liberal doctrine of the eighteenth and nineteenth centuries was based on the assumption that men are born "equal." If one means by this that all men are born endowed with equal abilities, it is nonsense. If one means that all men should be endowed with the same personal and political rights, one has to find a basis other than equal abilities for one's assump-

tion. This basis exists. Men are born not with
equal abilities but with an equal weakness.
All men are liable to make blunders. No person and no group of persons possesses a monopoly on infallibility. That is why in free countries citizens organize into parties and entrust
the government to that party whose leaders for
the time being inspire the most confidence. If
this party fails to justify the confidence placed
in it, another is put in its place. Justice Holmes
used to say that a democrat is a man who does
not believe himself to be the Almighty God.
Democracy is based on humility.

If, on the contrary, the gift of infallibility is
attributed to a man or a group of men, dictatorship by them becomes inevitable. In fact, if an
infallible god were to take over the care of our
welfare and happiness and map out faultless
five- or ten-year plans, the dictatorship of that
god would be the most suitable political regime
for carrying out his plans and for ensuring the
welfare of the people. Anyone opposing that
planning god would be either a fool or a wicked
enemy of public welfare. His opposition to the
infallible god would be an absurdity or a crime.
He should be put out of the way.

The philosophy of dictatorship is based on

the assumption that humanity is divided into two unequal parts: the mass, the "common herd," which knows and understands nothing; and a minority, the "chosen few," who alone know how to unravel all knots. "The best must rule the rest." But the "chosen few," the "best," have to be chosen by someone. This is the business of the dictator. "Authority comes from above." "Mussolini is always right," teaches the catechism of the perfect Fascist in Italy, and in Germany Göring proclaims: "We Nazis believe Adolf Hitler infallible in political affairs."

The Communist doctrine does not exalt one single man above all others but places above all other classes a collective entity, the proletariat. In actual fact, it is not the proletariat which exercises the rights of infallibility but the Communist Party and, above it, its supreme leader, Stalin. He has his own source of infallible inspiration — *Das Kapital* of Marx, and the teachings of Lenin.

In the Catholic Church — a perfectly organized religious dictatorship — the Pope is divinely inspired, and ordains the bishops, who, in their turn, ordain the priests. These, together, form the class of the "chosen few" to whom the faithful owe obedience: one God, one truth, one shepherd, and one flock to be guarded against sin and error.

The Catholic Church today is disarmed and consequently no longer burns heretics. It has to be satisfied with condemning them to eternal flames after they are dead. Stalin, Mussolini, and Hitler are armed. They control this world and not the next. What, for the Pope, constitutes a sin is for them a crime. And they sentence to death. He who is convinced that he possesses the infallible secret for making men happy is ever ready to kill them.

Dictatorial intolerance springs from the faith in infallibility in the same way that liberty and tolerance spring from democratic humility.

Scientists who deal with the facts of the physical world and social scientists who deal with phenomena of a comparatively simple nature are not seldom incapable of realizing the limitations of the human mind when confronted with the intricacies of social life. They are carried away by an unbridled confidence in the working of their own minds. Mathematics seems to be the most fertile breeding-ground for the mosquito of dogmatism when the mathematician shifts from his perfect science to the imperfect social sciences. Georges Sorel, Pareto, Spengler, Leon Trotsky, all came from mathematics to sociology or political activities, and all display to a high degree that habit of arrogant peremptoriness which may perhaps be suited to mathematics, where two and two are always four, but not to social life, where two and two may add up to three or five or even four.

The world today is overrun with experts who believe in their own infallibility and offer remedies for every social disease. Planning is necessary to regulate production and distribution in every country. International planning is necessary to regulate production and distribution in the world as a whole. Such planning cannot be carried out by any but experts. We unfortunate, wretched non-experts are commanded to bow before the infallible experts.

The infallible expert would perhaps become a little more restrained and humble if he realized that nobody can be an expert in everything. He who is an expert in producing motorcars may be wholly inexpert in handling problems of human behavior. The captain of a ship is the expert who knows how to navigate the ship, and the traveler must obey him throughout the voyage; but the traveler is the expert when it comes to knowing where he wants to go. Moreover, both the traveler and the captain are liable to make blunders in carrying out their respective jobs.

If one asks two experts to solve a technical problem, it is ten to one not only that they will not agree but also that neither of the two will admit that the other's solution might be better than his own. Both feel themselves infallible. It may also happen that the expert finds it convenient to make use of his knowledge not in the interests of the community but to replenish his own purse. Select a committee of experts to solve a problem of tariff, of taxation, of banking, and so on: under any type of government, whether democratic or dictatorial, half the experts are likely to be narrow-minded, one-sided, and stubborn specialists who "know more and more about less and less," and the other half agents of hidden interests. It would be a miracle to find among them a few broad-minded and disinterested men.

Experts are necessary to governments of all kinds, but they are a danger in governments of all kinds. Politicians are expert in one single capacity, that of handling men. A dictator is no more capable than the politician of democracy of judging beforehand the ability of his experts, nor does he know better beforehand what results the work of his experts will yield. He, too, must proceed by trial and error and await results, judging the tree by its fruit. Yet he claims to know positively what future generations — all the future generations to the end — expect from us; and it is on behalf of these generations as yet unborn that he imposes his will upon us.

People who wax enthusiastic over comprehensive planning always start from the implicit assumption of faultless planning. Never do they suspect that comprehensive planning may be equal to comprehensive blundering. Such optimism depends, perhaps, on the fact that they are sure that planning will never be planned against their own wishes, and, of course, they are convinced that their own wishes are flawless. They forget that the Almighty Himself had to acknowledge, one fine day, that he had blundered in his planned creation: he repented having made man and corrected that blunder by the Flood.

While the scientist who deals with the world

of exact sciences is not seldom afflicted with the virus of dogmatic and intolerant presumption, the historian and the social scientist are often afflicted with quite the opposite disease. Humility and tolerance degenerate into moral indifference.

Since each society, each social class in each society, and each individual in each social class has a different behavior, and since every human action can always be explained by its causes, the historian and the social scientist reach the conclusion that the only thing they have to do is to put themselves "beyond good and evil," take note of all existing human actions, and not only explain but also whitewash them as the necessary consequences of their conditioning antecedents. Born with a given temperament, the historian or the social scientist selects in the theater of life the place which best suits his temperament. He may sit in the orchestra to watch with curiosity what is taking place on the stage, without either applauding or hissing. This he calls "scientific detachment." Or else he may wait and see how things turn out and then rush to board the band wagon. It all depends on his temperament. He is tolerant in the sense that he possesses no moral backbone

of his own. He understands all principles and
has none. He does not eat his aged father or
mother, not because this would be immoral but
only because the society in which he lives has
discarded these practices; he would not object
to sharing in such a dinner were he visiting a
community of cannibals. Al Capone would
make a first-rate teacher of government. In
fact, no one could teach undergraduates and
graduates better than he "who gets, what, when,
how."

A characteristic controversy developed in the
International Quarterly of 1938 and 1939 between a social scientist and a scholar versed in
classical studies. The social scientist had made
a study of the German universities under Nazi
rule. In drawing up the balance sheet of gains
and losses, he had put the gains made by German youth through improvement in physical
health against the losses resulting for science
from the repression of intellectual freedom, and
he left the reader to draw his own conclusions.
The scholar whose mind had been formed by
the study of Aeschylus and Sophocles, of Seneca
and Tacitus, protested that this attitude showed
a deplorable inability to recognize radical evil.
The social scientist retorted that the task of the

social scientist is not that of passing judgments
on radical evil; the doctrines of evil are various;
therefore the social scientist regards ethical
judgments merely as data, without either agree-
ing or disagreeing with them. Even in his rebuttal he was careful to keep the detachment
of a social scientist, never letting it be known
whether or not in his opinion the losses which
science was suffering in Germany were an evil
which overbalanced the gains of youth in physical health. The classical scholar again came
forward, maintaining that a social scientist is
a human being and that no human being can
treat ethical judgments as "data" indifferent to
his moral conscience. If one were to say of a
corpse, "The man's vitality has of course been
impaired, but his beauty is enhanced by the
weird unearthly bloom of his dead face," one
would make a statement no whit more ethical
than the social scientist's judgment that there
are today much better physically equipped
Germans, which is a good thing, but, of course,
they are not allowed to think for themselves,
which is a bad thing, so let's make up our
minds which of these cancels out the other.

At the time of writing I do not know whether
the social scientist will make a second rebuttal.

But I am not a social scientist, and therefore I do not wait for that rebuttal in order to take sides with the classical scholar. I would go even further than he in fighting against the social scientist. I would say that it is not true that the social scientist did not possess standards of good or evil, and was only collecting "data." In stating that science in Nazi Germany had suffered "losses," he passed a "judgment" according to the principle that suppression of intellectual liberty is an evil. But by stating that science had suffered "losses" and yet had not been prostituted and denatured, he revealed that according to his standards a science which has become subservient to the party in power is still science, though a little damaged. Science was for him not something which by its very nature must not be controlled by any political authority or economic power, something which, therefore, when prostituted to such authorities or powers not only suffers "losses" but is completely denatured and is no longer science. In short, on this point the standards of the social scientist were nearer to Nazi standards than to liberal ones. Even when balancing the "gains" resulting from improved physical health against the "losses" of science, the social scientist was approaching a Nazi standard and was shrinking from another standard according to which mental degeneration is such an evil that no improvement in physical health can be balanced against it. Thus it is not true that the social scientist had no moral conscience. The truth is that he had a moral conscience which would allow him to teach social science in an American university today and in a Nazi university tomorrow. The old historians who candidly displayed their ethical judgments were more intelligent than those modern historians and social scientists who think that they avoid ethical judgments when they "objectively" balance "data" against "data" on scales which are swayed by the influence of unconscious ethical judgments, even if they themselves do not realize this fact.

I should be deeply distressed if, from the doctrine that history and the social sciences cannot provide us either with absolute truths or with secure previsions, any of my readers were to come to the conclusion that they must be indifferent to the question of truth or error, good or evil.

To be sure, prevision is, to a large extent, a gamble between possible issues. A mere trifle may upset every one of our forecasts. Often what happens is what no one had foreseen. Combinations of unpredictable factors may magnify to gigantic proportions the little which each one of us has contributed to the course of events. Who can say how far afield a seed cast on the wind will go, or how much it will yield? The actions and ideas of men are like seeds; after years and years of apparent sterility, they may spread with lightning rapidity.

Yet we must live. To live means to act. To act means to direct one's conduct towards results which are desired. Among the factors governing the future there are also our desires — that is, our intelligence and our will. Now, when we make a decision we are not solving a scientific problem, but we are performing an act with a moral bearing. History and the social sciences give us no moral guidance in deciding upon the aims we wish to attain by our actions. They merely supply hints concerning the choice of means necessary to the attainment of our aims. The mainspring of our decision is our moral personality. Even when we act with the certainty that our forecast will not be belied by future events, our choice has been determined not by that forecast but by a moral evaluation. The army chief decides on a certain plan of campaign not only because his calculations lead up to the hypothesis of victory but because, before making these calculations, he had resolved another problem not of a scientific but of a moral nature: he had decided that war, provided it ends in victory, is a moral, nay, a glorious action. The politician who inflates currency is convinced that such a measure is necessary to the country at large or to that social group whose interests he means to promote. He has given to a moral problem a moral or immoral solution.

One who is guilty of a dishonest or cowardly action is not entitled to exonerate himself with disingenuous scientific arguments; these arguments, as Pareto would say, are "derivations from a residue." Withdraw the derivations, and what remains at their root is not a scientific doctrine but a base character.

We have no certainty of possessing absolute truth in social questions. We are consequently bound not to ignore the points of view which stand in opposition to ours; we have not the right to suppress by violent means the views of others. In other words, we must respect the principle of reciprocal tolerance. But this is a juridical and not an intellectual or moral duty. To respect the juridical principle of tolerance does not mean to surrender to those who think differently from ourselves, nor to be ready to change our opinions like weathervanes in the wind. We and our opponents have the same juridical right to maintain our opinions, and the same juridical duty to respect that right in others. But we have no obligation to be intellectually tolerant of their errors or morally tolerant of their misdeeds. If we wish to preserve our self-respect, it is our intellectual right and our intellectual duty to maintain uncompromisingly our point of view, and to be intellectually intolerant of their error so long as they have not convinced us by sufficiently strong arguments that we are mistaken. Should they succeed in convincing us that we are mistaken, we must become intellectually or morally intolerant of our own error and instantly discard it.

Often we are told that we have to "understand" our adversary. No doubt we have to, but this is in order to know how more efficiently to combat his error, and not in order to make a hodgepodge composed of half his error and half our truth, or to give up our truth and swallow his error.

In conclusion, we will do well to "understand" "who gets, what, when, and how." But we must not fail to keep in mind that whoever gets what is not his due is a thief and a rascal, and that our civilization will break down if the school fails to teach the incoming generation that there are some things that are not done.

APPENDIX

WHAT IS CULTURE?

I. PROFESSIONAL CULTURE AND GENERAL CULTURE

THERE is great truth in that definition of culture according to which culture consists in "knowing something of everything and everything of something."

The man who knows everything about something, without knowing anything about all the rest, restricts his intellectual activities. He quenches in himself all curiosity outside the narrow circle of his speciality. He secludes himself from the world. He is the man of a single book, as our forefathers said. He cannot in any way be considered a man of culture. The specialist has killed the man. Our forefathers were wont to say *Mathematicus purus asinus purus:* The mathematician who knows nothing beyond his mathematics is a thorough ass.

Specialization is usually regarded as a professional malady peculiar to those who dedicate themselves to science, and particularly to university professors. But the banker, too, suffers from the same psychological deformity when he lives absorbed in the one preoccupation of growing rich, looking neither right nor left, piling up transaction upon transaction and wealth upon wealth, and completely stifling his inner life. So also does the judge who fits the whole human spirit into the code of legal procedure, and turns a cold eye upon the infinite welter of human miseries which life brings before him, intent only on classifying them according to the framework of the law. So does the engineer who seeks around him nothing but machines to construct, formulas to apply, and refractory materials to conquer, and forgets that behind the machines there are men who feel and think and suffer, and that men are not made for the machines but the machines to serve men. So does the military chief who in his barrack life regards the whole world as a barrack, and carries the habit of undisputed command and the need for immediate obedience into spheres where that habit and that need are out of place and even dangerous. These men, too, are one-sided specialists. A psychological deformation has taken place in them similar to that which as a rule is attributed to scientists alone.

To avoid the bad results produced on the inner life by excessive limitation of the intellectual range, we need, besides specialized and professional knowledge, a wide and varied stock of information of all kinds. In other words we must know something of everything, besides knowing everything of something. This nonprofessional culture we are led to acquire not by the desire to earn money but by a free and disinterested desire to cultivate our mind, to extend the field of our knowledge, and to live in addition to our own life the life of our fellows. We usually give the name of "general culture" to this not strictly professional knowledge, which is not intended to be turned into hard cash. Sometimes we call it "culture" pure and simple, as if to show that true culture does not consist in the knowledge we need in a special profession but begins precisely where professional utility ends.

For a day laborer the ability to read and write is culture. For the intellectual the ability to read and write is nothing: culture begins for him far beyond that. Knowledge which in a doctor is professional, and thus not a part of culture, becomes culture when it is found in the intellectual store of a lawyer. Vice versa, legal knowledge, which is culture for a doctor, does not imply in the lawyer any intellectual superiority or strength outside his profession. A friend of mine, a professor completely absorbed in the study of his special subject, was wont to say: "Culture is the luxury which my wife can afford herself."

Culture therefore is the sum of all that knowledge which serves no practical purpose but which one must possess if one wants to be a human being and not a specialized machine. Culture is the indispensable superfluity.

This stock of nonprofessional information which presumably serves no practical purpose needs to be organically arranged round that more solid nucleus of professional learning which is, so to speak, the personal property of the specialist. The man who has a smattering of everything and never concentrates his intellectual activities on a fixed point may perhaps score easy conversational triumphs; he succeeds better than the specialist in "cutting a good figure in society," as the expression is; but in the world of thought and the world of action he is utterly useless. He is not a man of culture; he is a parasite on the culture of others.

This is why we need not only to know something of everything but also everything of something.

II. THE RIGHT TO BE IGNORANT

On the other hand, the definition that culture consists in "knowing everything of something and something of everything" must be taken with many reservations.

In 1933 the professors of Princeton University, who so many times had subjected their pupils to intelligence tests, were in their turn subjected by their pupils to a test of the same nature. A questionnaire of forty-one statements drawn from all fields of knowledge — architecture, art and archeology, astronomy, biology, chemistry, the classics, economics, engineering, English, geology, history,

mathematics, military science, modern languages,
Oriental languages, philosophy, physics, politics,
psychology, geography, music, and "library" —
was submitted to twenty-five professors, who were
asked to mark each question "true" or "false."
The result of the test was disastrous for the professors. It showed "the inability of most modern
scholars to answer comparatively simple questions
outside their own fields. . . . Some of Princeton's
most distinguished teachers made lamentable
scores." [1]

If I had been one of the guinea pigs in that experiment, I should have made a very low score.
I should have been able to answer only twelve
questions, most of them relating to historical, economic, political, or artistic matters. To the other
twenty-nine questions I should have been unable
to give any answer. In many cases I should have
been unable even to understand the question.
Sentences like the following: "Recent developments in the manufacture of steel wire have em-
phasized the economy of cantilever as compared
with suspension bridges," or "The roots of a general polynomial of a degree higher than four are
not complete numbers," or "The four-dimensional
analogue of a cube has twelve corners," or "One
gram of methyl alcohol added to one kilogram of
water is more effective in lowering the freezing

[1] *Princeton Alumni Weekly,* April 7, 1933.

point than one gram of ethyl alcohol," were wholly above or below my understanding. Words might have slipped from one of these sentences into another, and I should not even have been aware of the confusion.

Yet I am not ashamed of my ignorance. A man cannot know everything. I am an historian by profession, and I have been a teacher of history for about fifty years; yet I am far from knowing everything about history. I possess a reasonably wide knowledge concerning about half a dozen groups of historical facts, which I have studied in the sources. Even of these facts, however, I cannot be said to know "everything." My colleagues say that I am an expert in these subjects, because I know more about them than the majority of historians and have brought to light facts which were formerly unknown, but even on these subjects there are facts immeasurably more numerous than those which I have succeeded in acquiring. Those who have carried on research after me in the same field have not found too great difficulty in surpassing my knowledge. This holds good only of the half dozen groups of historical facts which I have studied directly. Of most events of history I only know what is said in certain textbooks, and I shall never have either the opportunity or the time to go beyond the textbooks. Of many facts, again, I know nothing, or almost nothing. If I had to pass an examination in the history of the United States, I should certainly fail.

We shall never succeed in "knowing everything" even in the field of our professional culture, however hard we work, however great our powers of assimilation, and however narrow the limits which we lay down for our activities.

If it is beyond human powers to know everything about one thing, it is appalling to think what an immense burden of fatigue would be shouldered by the man who adopted the program of "knowing something about everything." The gaps in our culture, both general and professional, will always remain enormous. What one succeeds in learning and what one will never know stand in the proportions of a finite quantity to infinity: that is to say, our finite knowledge in relation to our infinite ignorance will always be equal to zero.

We are reluctant to recognize, in ourselves and in others, the necessity of being ignorant about an infinite number of things. We torment others and ourselves because we have neither the courage nor the humility to admit that our capacity to learn is and always will be limited, and that in these circumstances others as well as ourselves have the right of being and remaining ignorant of an infinite number of things. We think it "strange" that others do not know what we know, even if, on their part, they know a great many other things of which we are ignorant. We are a little like a certain lady I used to know, who read one novel a year, talked for the whole year about this novel, and regarded as ignorant those people who had not read her novel.

Our educational system often fails to recognize the right of youth to be ignorant about an infinite number of things.

If we examine one by one the different ways in which we have gathered the concrete facts of which our personal culture is today built up, we realize that very few of them came to us from school; and, vice versa, that we have forgotten in the course of our life much of the knowledge once imparted to us at school. The facts which we possess today have been acquired by us since our school days, in our daily experience of life, in reading books and reviews, listening to public lectures, conversing and discussing various subjects with friends, going to the theater or cinema, looking at advertisements and reading the papers — especially in reading the daily papers, which, with all their inaccuracies and shortcomings, are today the most effective and economical disseminators of varied knowledge.

Look into yourselves for a moment; and think of all the information about hygiene, legal procedure, international history, art, science, etc., you absorb every day, without any effort, by reading a

good newspaper. Even if your only object is to
answer a crossword puzzle, you are obliged to
search out a wide mass of information: you must
consult dictionaries and encyclopedias; you must
call upon the culture of your friends to help you
in interpreting metaphors and allusions. These
are many new materials which increase your
knowledge.

No school can impart all the knowledge which
may be necessary, useful, or pleasant in life. What
the school can give is a small number of clear and
well-coördinated facts and ideas, capable of serving
as a framework into which to fit the further experiences of life. After we leave school unexpected
information reaches us day by day throughout the
whole course of our life. This unexpected information acquires meaning and value only as it fits
into the framework of the knowledge gained at
school. The school gives us keys to open locks and
compasses to guide us on the sea of life. It
teaches us to be on our guard against unlikely or
false statements. It gives us a sense of proportion
and perspective. It prepares our thought to receive,
little by little, the seeds which will afterwards
bear fruit. It instills into us the taste for learning
and the discipline of study. It teaches us how to
learn for ourselves whenever the need or the opportunity arises. Had our schools not given us this
intellectual discipline, the heterogeneous notions

we pick up day by day in after life would remain so much indigestible material, never to be assimilated. They would be not culture but scattered and useless breadcrumbs.

Unfortunately, education is too often based on the prejudice that the pupil will never learn anything in his life after he has left school, and that therefore he must learn at school everything which may be in some way necessary, or indeed merely useful, to him in life. The newspapers are full of complaints about the inefficiency of the schools. One day some well-intentioned person mourns that in the schools of a given city the history of that city is not part of the curriculum. Another day some educator proposes that on the senior high school level the boys and girls shall be instructed in social finance, family budgeting, installment planning, taxation, and government. On still another day someone despairs because the "nation's children are unable to carry on government," and therefore suggests that they shall be obliged to study sociology, social psychology, and current events. On another day we are told that boys and girls should be taken at the age of ten and instructed in aviation until they are eighteen. Another day cries of despair arise because twenty-seven per cent of the pupils do not know "the number of churches," forty-three per cent do not know "how many newspapers" there are, and only

about a fifth know "the local death rate and the
average annual rainfall" in their community. Besides being instructed in these indispensable matters, high school students should be versed also in
"questions involving nationalism, internationalism,
race, and politics" and should be informed on "the
total breadth of various social sciences." [2] The
students themselves are convinced that it is their
right to be taught everything in school and that
after leaving school they will no longer learn anything. While I am taking a last glance at these
pages, I read that two hundred Harvard students
have signed a petition asking for a "special practical guidance course" in marriage. Evidently they
do not expect any practical knowledge from their
personal experience after leaving school, when it
comes to choosing their wives. At the same time
everybody complains that the colleges are sending
out many graduates who cannot write their mother
tongue.

I have no quarrel either with aviation or with
the science of government or of marriage, and even
less with writing one's mother tongue. I only ask,
"What are the other subjects that the high school
student will be allowed to ignore in order to find
time to study aviation, marriage, the total breadth
of various social sciences, and the rest?" There
are only twenty-four hours in a day. How many

[2] *New York Times*, Jan. 24, 1939.

hours a day must the high school student devote to study? Everything cannot be crowded into those hours, whatever they may be. You cannot expect a boy or girl to know aviation, government, the science of marriage, the history of his own town, etc., and at the same time expect him to know how to write correct and forceful English. There is not time for everything. One has to choose. If boys and girls are to acquire a thorough knowledge of English, the science of marriage, aviation, and the rest must be postponed to a more appropriate time. On the other hand, why should boys and girls devote their youth to learning to carry on government? How many university professors reach the age of eighty without knowing anything about family budgeting and installment planning?

The result of the fatal misconception that education consists in encyclopedic knowledge crammed in at school is that the pupils are overburdened, bewildered, and suffocated by an incoherent mass of facts, which are often at loggerheads among themselves, and which the pupils must have at the tips of their tongues, ready to repeat them parrot-wise. The soul, as Plutarch said, is not a vessel to be filled but a fire to be kindled. This fire is not kindled by crushing the spirit under the dead weight of material facts and stuffing it with an unassimilated medley of encyclopedic knowledge.

No wonder, therefore, if more than a third of the pupils in the seventh grade answer that "habeas corpus" is a disease — an answer that would put them at the top of their class in Nazi Germany or Fascist Italy; if one out of ten defines "habeas corpus" as a lawyer—which in truth is not far from the mark; and if one out of every ten defines poverty as "the boyhood of great men," while five per cent of the seniors, having become better acquainted with the realities of life, answer that poverty is an "unhappy state." [3] They have had no time to think, reflect, or assimilate. They have acquired neither a solid groundwork of facts nor soundness of judgment. They are incapable of analyzing, abstracting, associating, and coördinating ideas. Of this kind of education Oscar Wilde was thinking, probably, when he stated that "people are made stupid by education." They have studied every conceivable thing; but the result of all this labor is that nothing remains in their minds except a violent dislike of study. They graduate in order to have done with studying, as some men take a wife in order to do away with love.

The evil is in this, not in the fact that young people do not know how many churches there are and what the rainfall is in their respective communities. If I were a meteorologist or a farmer, the

[3] *New York Times,* Jan. 24, 1939.

knowledge of the average annual rainfall in my community would form a necessary element in my professional equipment, and I should be a fool if I were ignorant of such an important piece of information. But since I am an historian by trade I may without great disadvantage remain in ignorance concerning that phenomenon, so important for meteorologists and farmers. Of course I should not feel ashamed if I knew not only the average annual rainfall but also the death rate, the birth rate, the number of churches, newspapers, motorcars, deaf-mutes, and telegraph poles, and many other numbers not only in my community but in all communities of the world. I should like to know everything about everything. But this is impossible; I have to give up many things. I start with giving up the rainfall. The only thing about rainfall I need to know is that when it rains I must take an umbrella — and this I did not learn at school.

To achieve good results, the school must not attempt to teach either everything on something or something on everything; it must not over-burden and weary the brain with encyclopedic knowledge: it must recognize the right of the young to be ignorant.

III. INTELLECTUAL CULTURE

What then is culture?

To answer this question, let us observe how a man with a highly specialized training, say a physician, behaves if he is at the same time a man of culture.

However great may be his medical knowledge, he does not know medicine in the sense of having always present in his memory all the innumerable possible maladies which may torment the human race. He recognizes at first sight and knows how to treat immediately only those diseases, which occur most commonly in the practice of his profession. In addition he knows that there exist diseases which present different symptoms from those about which he has most experience. When he is confronted with one of such cases, he reserves his opinion before giving a definite verdict. He returns to his books. He returns again to observe the patient. When he is sure of what he says, he gives his opinion. The difference between the great physician and the mediocre or incompetent practitioner does not lie in the former's knowing everything and the latter's knowing very little. The former also knows very little in the face of the infinite number of facts which constitute the doctrine and practice of medicine, but he is capable of facing new problems whenever the necessity or

the desire arises, and despite the gaps in his learning; whereas the second not only knows very little
but is incapable of dealing with unexpected difficulties. A further difference between the cultured
physician and the practitioner who cares about
nothing beyond his professional round is that the
former, with his wide range of outside interests,
remains intellectually fresh and vigorous long after
his colleague has fallen victim to professional
somnambulism and lost all human contact with his
fellows.

If knowledge of history means the ability to repeat the whole of history by heart, nobody, not
even the greatest historian, knows history. But he
knows that he does not know the whole of history,
and this is already a great deal. Moreover, he is
capable of studying and understanding historical
facts whenever the desire or the necessity arises.
This is what is really important. In addition, he
knows that reality is something infinitely more vast
and complex than the field of his own profession,
and he tries to keep the doors and windows of his
mind open towards the unforeseen contingencies
of life. This is more important than his professional and nonprofessional knowledge.

To put the matter in a nutshell, culture consists
not in the mass of raw material stored in memory
but in the capacity of the mind to be always on the
alert, to be rich in curiosity about varied fields, and

to be able, when necessary, to acquire new knowledge. Culture is the habit of clear and logical thinking, is the courage of independent judgment. "Culture is what remains in our mind after we have forgotten everything we have learned."

Although culture consists not so much in concrete knowledge as in a capacity to master facts and organize them in our minds, we must not conclude that there is a contradiction between knowledge and culture, between learning and understanding. Understanding cannot be achieved without acquiring at the same time a wide knowledge of concrete facts, both professional and non-professional. A well-formed brain is always a well-stocked brain. Every new bit of information, on entering the mind which has habits of order and clarity, is at once illumined, vivified, and enriched by associating itself with already acquired notions which the well-stocked and agile mind brings into play. No idea is ever formulated without immediately becoming a nucleus around which are coordinated other ideas and experiences. Thus, abundance of information is the natural result of true "culture."

But anybody who aims at this result must give up the illusion of being able to learn everything. If one studies history with the sole purpose of hurriedly wiping out the disgrace of one's ignorance, one will read the first book as quickly as possible so as to acquire the greatest possible mass of information; but behind the first book there is another book waiting to be read; and behind that, another awaits reproachfully. Never a moment's rest or relaxation. The result is that the mind wears itself out and exhausts itself with a burden of indigested knowledge. The delicate mechanism of the mind threatens to break down without even increasing its store of concrete facts.

Knowledge acquired in frantic haste soon fades from the memory, because memory, as a rule, retains facts and ideas only when they are logically coördinated. Even if memory is so tenacious that it never forgets a thing once acquired, these hurried and haphazard acquisitions do not constitute culture; they add nothing to the strength, beauty, or refinement of the mind. At the most, they turn the brain into a secondhand shop.

A history book is to be studied not with the aim of stuffing the memory with facts but with that of training the mind to observe the complexity of the social structure, the continuity of historical processes, the relativity of institutions and ideas, and the relations of cause and effect which bind together social phenomena, whether past or contemporary.

To read a book properly, one must take time over it and meditate on it at leisure. Meanwhile one must give up the idea of studying many other books. In this way one's culture will rest on a comparatively small number of facts. But these facts will be a lasting possession, because they are not scattered and inorganic fragments. They form a compact system, firmly joined by intimate logical ties to all the other elements of one's culture. One will never be able to recall to one's mind a single part of the knowledge so well mastered without immediately witnessing the effortless revival of all the other parts. After a year, or five, or ten, the concrete facts thus acquired will drop from one's memory as the autumn leaves fall one by one from the tree. Other facts will take their place and will in their turn fall into oblivion and make way for others. But they will leave the mind with a greater intellectual agility, a more vigorous, plastic, and widely ranging thought. This will be the permanent gain to culture.

Study is for the intelligence what gymnastics are for the body. In gymnastic exercises the immediate results have a practical value only for the professional who has specialized in a definite branch of athletics with the purpose of earning money in matches. The great majority of those who play games do not seek financial profit from them but only physical culture pure and simple. You row for the sheer pleasure of the exercise and also because afterwards your body is better balanced and your muscles more fully developed.

Study is not so delightful as rowing. But even the learning to row is not all pleasure in the beginning. It is only when the beginner has got over the first ache of his unaccustomed muscles that rowing becomes a pleasure. Study, too, once the habit is formed, becomes a source of delight. And, besides its immediate results, it enriches us with a further gain which is still more precious: it makes the mind stronger and renders it capable of new efforts and conquests.

Imagine a boy struggling with a foreign text which he does not understand. Before being able to translate it, he has to put forth all the faculties of his mind to grasp the thought of the author. Memories of grammar and vocabulary alone are not enough. Reason must supply the guiding thread. Where memory and reason fall short, imagination must step into the breach with hypotheses, as in scientific research. Results known to be certain must become starting points or checks for new hypotheses. In laying bare the thoughts of others, the boy learns to probe his own thoughts; when he comes to the work of translation he must summon to his aid all the subtleties of his own mother tongue, in order to reproduce as closely as possible ideas which are nearly always expressed in a manner foreign to his native idiom. At the end of all this toil he has nothing to show but one poor wretched page of translation. The uneducated and superficial observer, seeing nothing beyond this meager return, regards the hours spent in wrestling with these difficulties as sheer waste of the boy's time, and thinks to himself how much better this time might have been spent in learning to set up a wireless apparatus or in organizing an advertising campaign which should induce millions of men and women to masticate a new brand of chewing-gum. From the point of view of an immediate financial return, it is obvious that the boy has been wasting his time. But in making this apparently useless effort he awakes and refines his critical acumen. He grows used to observing methodically, thinking clearly and logically, and expressing himself with order and precision. He becomes a man of heightened reasoning powers.

IV. AESTHETIC AND MORAL CULTURE

Intellectual culture is not the only aspect of culture. Every human being is a bundle of possibilities not only intellectual but also aesthetic and moral. Alongside of intellectual culture there also exist an aesthetic culture and a moral culture.

When we listen to a symphony by Beethoven, or gaze at Botticelli's "Venus Rising from the Sea," or read Shelley's *Prometheus Unbound,* we are doing nothing to increase our balance at the bank, supposing we have one. No doubt these are opportunities for us to increase our stock of knowledge by learning that there once existed a certain Beethoven who was a composer of music, that Venus was a fair goddess of ancient Greece, and that Prometheus came to a bad end because he wanted to know too much. But, if that is all, we should have done better to turn to an encyclopedia. The work of art is not made to increase our erudition. It is there to give us joy, to refine our taste, to heighten our vital energy, to enrich our experience. This explains why we return again and again to the same work of art without ever growing tired of it, without ever feeling that it is a waste of time. This is aesthetic culture.

Let us now read that short poem of Kipling's entitled "If." After reading it, we are none the wiser about the way the Britishers founded their empire or how many inhabitants it contains. But we do feel that our own energies, our courage to face new problems of thought and action, and our powers of rapid decision and firm purpose have been heightened. This is moral culture. Tolstoy's *Resurrection* does not give us one single item of information which is of the slightest practical utility. Even from the point of view of aesthetic value, *Resurrection* is far from being the finest of Tolstoy's works. And yet, when we read it, something most profound and unforgettable enters our souls. We become conscious of all our own moral ugliness, of all those failings which we have never confessed to anyone else, and hardly acknowledge to ourselves; but at the same time we are lifted to moral heights of which before we had never dreamed. Our spirit is swept along by a magnificent wave of desire for goodness. Alas, we cannot maintain ourselves always on that level. We lack the heroism of the great. But, for having even once touched those heights, we are never quite the same again after we return to our everyday life. Something remains in our innermost selves which will never be entirely lost. This is moral culture.

Most boys would prefer a jolly walk in the company of friends to attending school. Yet they have to go to school; and by doing so they accustom themselves to realize that life is not made up only of pleasure, and that there are pleasures which one must give up in order to do work which one should like to escape. To wake up at a given hour, to arrive on time at school, to obey the rules which regulate conduct in school, all this is not pleasant, may even be regarded as a burden at moments. But through the sacrifices which are needed in the daily life at school the boy acquires habits of order and discipline indispensable in after life. This is moral culture. The dogged effort to which our school years accustom us, besides giving us invaluable intellectual habits, also forms in us certain moral habits of industry, tenacity, self-control, which are infinitely more essential in after life than any acquisition of concrete knowledge and any degree of intellectual refinement.

The difficulties of certain studies are simply a foretaste of the far greater difficulties of life. A certain number of failures at school are all to the good if the experience of failure teaches the young person to avoid more disastrous and irreparable failures in after life. Life after all is but a series of examinations which cannot be taken a second time.

We have the right to be ignorant. We have no right to be lazy. Our ignorance must be a conscious ignorance, eager to conquer itself, and not a complacent, resigned ignorance. We must not passively accept it, like oxen chewing the cud. But the capacity to overcome our ignorance whenever necessity arises is not acquired without strenuous effort. "In the sweat of thy brow shalt thou earn thy bread." Culture is the bread of the soul. It is not found readymade in the cradle. We must toil and suffer to acquire and preserve it.

This means that the foundation of a solid intellectual culture is to be found in a strong moral character. However fine an intellect may be, it will never produce its fruit unless coupled with sufficient strength of character; and, conversely, a powerful will can achieve great things with an intelligence of only mediocre quality.

The human spirit cannot be cut up in slices. We

can never say: "Now by this exercise we are going to educate the mind, and by this other exercise we are going to train the character." Every intellectual effort is at the same time a training of character. And, conversely, we cannot conceive of any moral endeavor unaccompanied by an effort of intelligence.

Even the physical culture attained by games, when not carried to such excess that it leaves no room for intellectual culture, is of indirect benefit to the mind, in that it brings rest and a respite from books and gives the mind time to recover freshness and vigor for further labors. When it does not degenerate into brutality, as in boxing or bullfighting, sport is a most valuable factor in the formation of character in so far as it teaches self-control, coöperation, subordination of self to the good of the team, fair play towards the adversary, modesty in success, courage and good humor in defeat.

Physical culture, intellectual culture, aesthetic culture, and moral culture are the different aspects of human culture. The ideal human personality is attained by the balanced development of all four. What human society needs is that its members should have healthy bodies, well-stocked and alert minds, refined tastes, and well-disciplined characters. But in the long run what the community most needs is moral culture. If one aspect is to be stressed at the expense of the others, then it should be that of moral culture.

A French novelist, Jean Aicard, in his novel *Maurin des Maures,* tells the story of an unlettered man of the people who takes his eleven-year-old son to a pensioned naval surgeon with the request to give the lad a bit of schooling. "What do you want me to teach him?" asks the surgeon. "I don't know. But I want him not to be like me, hardly able to read. I am nothing better than a savage." "I see. Does the boy know how to read?" "Yes, he has learnt the three R's." "Well, what do you want to turn him to?" The father could not find a reply. "But surely you have some plan or other for the lad's future. Do you want him to be a farmer, or a soldier, or a sailor, or a hunter, or a gardener? According as you decide, I will try to adapt my teaching." After a long hesitation the father finally found what he wanted: "Teach him justice." The common sense of this man of the people, ignorant but intelligent and morally sound, realized that it was futile to decide what a boy of eleven was to do when he grew up. The boy would get his specialized training by himself later on when he was old enough to know his own mind. But one thing he would need, more essential than an intellectual culture extending beyond the three R's. That was a moral training that would make him grow up an honest man.

So let us conclude with the words of this un-lettered man, who, though he thought himself nothing better than a savage, was more civilized than most of the men who pass for such. Develop your intellectual, aesthetic, and physical culture, but above all learn "justice."

INDEX

INDEX